a youth worker's commentary on JAMES

jas

a youth
worker's
commentary
on
JAMES

david nystrom & les christie

ZONDERVAN

A Youth Worker's Commentary on James
Copyright © 2013 by Les Christie and David Nystrom

YS Youth Specialties is a trademark of YOUTHWORKS!, INCORPORATED and is registered with the United States Patent and Trademark Office.

This title is also available as a Zondervan ebook.
Visit www.zondervan.com/ebooks.

Requests for information should be addressed to:

Zondervan, *Grand Rapids, Michigan 49530*

Library of Congress Cataloging-in-Publication Data

Nystrom, David P., 1959 –
    A youth worker's commentary on James / David Nystrom, Les Christie.
      pages cm.
    Includes bibliographical references.
    ISBN 978-0-310-67034-6 (softcover)
    1. Bible. James—Study and teaching 2. Bible. James—Criticism, interpretation, etc.
  3. Church work with youth. I. Christie, Les John. II. Title.
  BS2785.55.N97 2013
  227'.91077 – dc23   2013023590

Cover design: Chris Gilbert, Gearbox
Interior design: David Conn and Ben Fetterley

Printed in the United States of America

13 14 15 16 17 18 19 /DCI/ 22 21 20 19 18 17 16 15 14 13 12 11 10 9 8 7 6 5 4 3 2 1

CONTENTS

128 939

ACKNOWLEDGMENTS

We are grateful to Jay Howver, former publisher of Youth Specialties, for his positive response to our book's initial proposal. We are appreciative of Greg Clouse, senior editor of Zondervan's book group, for coordinating all of the components that go into the publishing process. We are indebted to our editor, Dave Urbanski, who took our original manuscript and shaped it with great care into a more cohesive book. Thanks also to Tammy Johnson for her thought-provoking cover design, to David Conn for his work on the interior design, to Andrew Rogers for marketing the book, and to Laura Gross and Heather Haggerty for their *careful proofreading*.

INTRODUCTION [AND HOW TO USE THIS BOOK]

This single-volume commentary on the letter of James is designed to reach and engage the hearts and minds of youth workers and their students. Our hope is that you will find it stimulating as you seek to unpack ancient biblical truth in today's world. Written with the busy youth worker in mind, our desire is that you find this book an invaluable aid in saving you time while preparing lessons and messages. You can also use this book for personal reading and edification, but the commentary's primary purpose is to stimulate small group discussions that will help you and your students grow in faith and knowledge of God and the Scriptures.

As in previous volumes in this series, we'll walk you through the letter of James a few verses at a time, thoughtfully considering the context and meaning of each element in James' narrative. In each episode we'll take a rich look into the rationale and meaning of the text, including word, personal, and historical context studies. At the end of each section of verses, you'll find a group of thought-provoking discussion questions to help get your students thinking and talking and connecting the biblical text with their world.

We hope you'll move through James at a pace that best suits you and your group. You may want to do an episode a week for a few weeks, and then take a break from James and come back to it again later. Or, if you think your group could handle it, you could go through the entire letter of James, all 21 episodes. Or, you may want to select particular episodes from different sections of James.

When using the book in small group discussions, we recommend having a student read aloud a small portion of the text or the entire passage you'll be tackling. Ask the group what key words stood out and have them highlight those words in their text and note any observations. Then discuss some of the Read Between the Lines questions at the end of each study—they invite your students to dig more deeply into the text. You don't have to use every question; just pick a few that might appeal to you or your group. Toward the end of your session, move into the Welcome to My World questions that invite students to apply what they've learned, bringing the study home to where they live, work, and play.

James and His Letter

James is something of an oddity among New Testament books—it's difficult to categorize and elicits a wide variety of descriptions. The text is simple and straightforward, marked by ethical teaching and authoritative statements—but it seems to lack (at first glance) sustained theological arguments. These factors, in part, led Martin Dibelius to conclude that James is a jumbled series of unrelated bits of teaching material strung together. But Fred Francis has argued that the epistle is actually a carefully constructed document which conforms to established patterns.

The letter is addressed to a generic audience—"the twelve tribes scattered among the nations" (1:1)—rather than a specific church, as are so many of Paul's letters. The difficulties that James addresses likely touched many different early Christian communities.

First, it's clear that the letter of James can be placed within the context of the earliest forms of Christianity. For instance:

- There are numerous, striking parallels to Jesus' teaching in the synoptic Gospels—and seemingly in concert with the earliest texts. Perhaps the best example is James 5:12, which closely resembles

Jesus' words concerning oaths in Matthew 5:33-37. Therefore it is plausible that James had contact with an early source of Jesus' sayings—perhaps the same source(s) the synoptic Gospel writers (especially Matthew) had at their disposal.

- Many other parallels between James and the synoptic Gospels bolster this conclusion: Believers are to rejoice in trials (James 1:2; Matthew 5:12); believers are called to be perfect/complete (James 1:4; Matthew 5:48); believers are encouraged to ask God, for God loves to give (James 1:5; Matthew 7:7); believers should expect testing and be prepared to endure it, after which they will receive a reward (James 1:12; Matthew 24:13); believers are not to be angry (James 1:20; Matthew 5:22); the poor are blessed (James 2:5; Luke 6:20); faith and action go together—in fact, actions are the proof of true faith (James 2:14; Matthew 7:16-19); the rich are warned (James 2:6-7; Matthew 19:23-24); the humble are praised (James 3:13; Matthew 5:3); believers are not to slander (James 4:11; Matthew 5:22); believers are not to judge (James 4:12; Matthew 7:1).
- Both James and Paul are concerned with the relationship between faith and works, and while it's probably wrong to read James as a reaction against Paul, James' conclusions demonstrate his Christian environment—even the date, perhaps. (Again, James appears to be a very early document.)
- When James calls Jesus "glorious" in 2:1, it's difficult to miss the Christological path that also surfaces in the Gospel of John.

In short, there is ample evidence that James belongs to the world of the earliest forms of the Christian faith.

Second, James is familiar with Judaism. While James

is unquestionably a Christian book, its roots in Judaism are deep:

- His picture of God is compatible with the Jewish understanding. He knows that "there is one God" (2:19). He knows the importance of the terms "Almighty" (5:4) and "Father" (3:9) used in reference to God. He teaches that God is merciful (4:8), and that he desires purity and humility in his people (4:8, 10). He is aware that the world tends to work in ways that oppose God and his intentions (4:4). Finally, he knows that God desires to give (4:2).

- James is aware of other characteristic features of the beliefs of first-century Judaism. He knows the term "Gehenna" often meant satanic power (3:6). He is aware of rabbinic theological and psychological anthropology, specifically the belief in the *yesarim*—the two impulses in each of us (1:14). (The first is pure or the "good impulse" [yeser ha-tov], while the second is the "evil impulse" [yeser ha-ra].) James knows that within first-century Judaism the poor had become associated with the righteous (2:5; 4:6). Finally, he knows about the perfect law, the law of the love of one's neighbor as found in Leviticus 19:18 (1:25; 2:8).

- James frequently quotes and alludes to the Old Testament. He makes reference to what "Scripture says" (4:5) and even quotes the Old Testament (4:6). His concern for widows and orphans (1:27) shows his familiarity with the prophetic notion of justice. Further, he refers to the great Old Testament heroes of the faith such as Abraham (2:23), Rahab (2:25), the prophets (5:10), and Job (5:11).

But on the other hand, James is no stranger to the Hellenistic world:

- The letter is written in fluid Greek using a wide vocabulary, word plays, and figures of speech. Yet it avoids complex words and sentences that mark the highest Greek literature.
- The letter shows an interest in Greek oral composition, using alliteration and rhyme.
- A number of metaphors are drawn from the Hellenistic Mediterranean world, which would have been lost on those from Palestine.

In short, James displays a Christian context, Jewish roots, and an aim toward the multilingual Mediterranean Hellenistic culture of the eastern Roman provinces.

In addition, the epistle of James is very practical (not an unfamiliar observation). That said, one challenge for those of us who want to learn from it is ignoring its practicalities in favor of overly academic concerns or self-righteous reinterpretation.

We need to allow James to make us uncomfortable, for his message bears eternal consequences.

Authorship

We aren't certain of the identity of James (a common name in the first century). The letter is notoriously restrained in yielding clues concerning the traditional questions of authorship, date, and addressees.

There are three basic options to answer the question of authorship:

1. That James is a pre-Christian Jewish document that was embraced by one of the infant Christian communities. According to champions of this position, the author and editor(s) are unknown. Supporters of this position cite the concern with deeds as evidence of the letter's Jewish origin. Further, the many

features revealing the letter's comfort with the Old Testament and other typically Jewish themes are said to support this view. But this position is becoming increasingly difficult to maintain.

2. The epistle was composed in two stages. Ralph Martin believes it originated with the teaching of James, the brother of Jesus, who was martyred by the High Priest Ananus II in about AD 62. Martin believes that after the Jewish War of AD 66-70, James' community left Palestine and settled in Syria. There they refined the teachings of James that they possessed and created a final product—the letter we know as James.

3. James, the brother of the Lord, wrote the letter. There are several persons named James mentioned in the New Testament. They include:

   - James, the brother of Jude (Jude 1);
   - James, the father of Judas (not Iscariot) (Luke 6:16);
   - James, "the younger" (Mark 15:40);
   - James, the son of Zebedee, the brother of John (Mark 1:19, 3:17); a strong contender for author, but his early martyrdom (Acts 12:2) seems to rule him out;
   - James, the son of Alphaeus, one of the original 12 disciples (Mark 3:18; Matthew 10:2-3), and possibly the same person listed as James "the younger";
   - James, the son of Joseph and half-brother of Jesus (Galatians 1:19), also known as "James the Just."

There's no reason to suppose that James the brother of Jesus is not the author of this epistle. Further, references to James by Paul (1 Corinthians 9:5, 14; 15:7; Galatians

1:15-2:12) and Acts (15:13-21) make clear that James the brother of Jesus held a prominent place in early Christianity. Origen (AD 185- 251) mentions the letter and claims it was written by James the brother of Jesus.

Still, one of the difficulties with this view is the scarceness of references to James by the early church fathers relative to the other books in the New Testament canon. Eusebius (AD 266-339) agrees with Origen that James the brother of Jesus wrote the letter, and it was "read publicly in many churches," but Eusebius adds that some in his own day doubted the same James is the author.

Today the view that James the brother of Jesus wrote the letter in a form substantially as we have it is not popular—but it's still highly likely that James the brother of Jesus wrote the letter, or at the very least its teaching originated with him.

Imagine growing up in a family with Jesus as your brother. Mary and Joseph certainly knew who Jesus was. It stands to reason that they explained Jesus' true identity to the rest of the family. But James and the others (including Jude, the author of the book of Jude) remained unconvinced: "For even his own brothers did not believe in Him" (John 7:5).

But a few years later, this same James became the leader of the church in Jerusalem (Acts 12:17; 15:1-21). What changed James from a skeptical younger brother to a committed follower of Jesus and outspoken leader of the Jerusalem church? The best answer is that James saw Jesus alive three days after he was crucified and buried in a tomb (1 Corinthians 15:3-8).

According to Josephus, a first-century Jewish historian, James was condemned to death by the Jewish Sanhedrin in AD 62, just after the death of the Roman governor Festus (Acts 24:27-26:32).

Many believe the letter of James was written early in the

life of the church about AD 47-49. Reasons for the early date include the early death of James. Also there is no mention of the Jewish/Gentile controversy of the fifties and sixties, and there is no mention of the apostle Paul or his writings.

The Teaching of James

James wrote to a church overwhelmed by problems—including divisiveness, intolerance, favoritism, and the desire for wealth and status. Giving shape to and stirring these up was the presence and popularity of errant teaching that questioned the Great Commandment (Deuteronomy 6:5; Levitiucus 19:18) as expressed by Jesus (Matthew 22:37-39) and yet maintaining its place in the community.

Tailor-made for the time, this wayward teaching allowed its adherents to view the church as a social ladder and stage for snobbery. Perhaps the most troublesome result of this teaching was that it divided the wealthy (and those who desired riches) from the poor in the community.

James combats this teaching and its effects by calling for true Christian community. He points out that the rich will be humbled and the poor exalted; that the poor are God's elect; that far from being a sign of divine displeasure, periods of adversity are used by God to purify and strengthen those he loves.

Also James makes crystal clear his assertion that friendship with the world is enmity with God (4:4). In other words, those who want it both ways are the double-minded, and James warns that this foolishness has unpleasant and eternal consequences. Still he points to the forgiveness of God if only they will repent.

Introduction and Greeting

James 1:1a

1a James, a servant of God and of the Lord Jesus Christ,

Most letters from antiquity and in the New Testament are generally familiar in tone. They also follow an established pattern or order:

1. The name of the sender;
2. The name of the recipient;
3. A word of greeting, usually a blessing or the expression of a desire for good health;
4. The body of the letter;
5. The closing.

Like other examples in the New Testament, James has altered slightly the standard formula by adding theologically important terms and including in his opening a summary of the main themes of the letter.

The letter begins with a claim to be written by James (Matthew 13:53-55; Acts 1:12-14; 15:12-21; 1 Corinthians 15:3-8; Galatians 1:19; 2:7-9). As we have seen, there is no viable reason to doubt that James the brother of Jesus is the source for this letter.

It is, however, remarkable that James does not begin by saying he is the brother of the Lord Jesus Christ and a leader in the Jerusalem church. It could be that James is a humble person, referring to himself simply as a "servant" (*doulos*). There is little agreement among the commentators as to his intended meaning. Perhaps it is best to explore the full range of possibilities.

Doulos was the common Greek term for "slave," although it could also be translated as "servant." Our understanding of this term is heavily and unfortunately colored by the experiences of recent history, a model that bears almost no resemblance to slavery in the Roman Empire. This is true for at least two reasons: First, Roman slavery had little if anything to do with race; second, Roman slavery was far more complex than its modern counterpart, encompassing four major types:

1. The most scandalous form was slavery in the mines, normally reserved for criminals or others judged as enemies of Rome. Life expectancy was low for this type of slave. Christian communities cared for believers condemned to the mines as noted by Eusebius in his *Ecclesiastical History* (4.23.10) where he relates that Dionysius, bishop of Corinth around AD 170, wrote a letter to Soter, the bishop of Rome. In it Dionysius commended the Roman church for its generosity in sending contributions to churches in many cities, thereby "relieving the poverty of the needy and ministering to the Christians in the mines."

2. Rural slavery is documented in the agricultural manuals of Columella, Cato, and Varro, which describe its harsh conditions: Work was performed in chain gangs, family life existed at the whim of the slave owners, and rations could be cut to the bare minimum for slaves when they fell ill.

3. The slavery that the New Testament refers to most often is urban household slavery. Here conditions also varied, but we do know of cases where people actually sold themselves into slavery because new masters typically provided food, shelter, and often training in a skill.

First Clement 55:2 asserts that some Christians had sold themselves into slavery in order to secure the ransom of other enslaved Christians: "We know of many among ourselves who have given themselves up to bonds, in order that they might ransom others. Many, too, have surrendered themselves to slavery, that with the price which they received for themselves, they might provide food for others." Paul speaks against this practice in 1 Corinthians 7:23, "You were bought at a price; do not become slaves of human beings."

Many scholars believe that urban household slaves could expect *manumission* (i.e., the process by which a slave was legally set free) after only a few years of service; some argue it was nearly automatic by the age of 30. Manumission could come in a variety of forms, including the awarding of a sum of money to the freed or even adoption by the master. This helps enlighten New Testament injunctions of slaves to "please" their masters (Ephesians 6:5-8; Colossians 3:22-25; 1 Timothy 6:1-2; Titus 2:9-11) and perhaps even for masters to "provide your slaves with what is right and fair" (Colossians 4:1; Ephesians 6:9).

A letter from a freedman to his former owner in Egypt in 14 BC provides an interesting parallel: "You know in your heart that I have behaved in a manner which is beyond reproach, wanting your goodwill, just as a slave wants to please in the interests of securing his freedom."

—*Berliner Griechische Urkunden, Ägyptisch Urkinden aus den Koniglichen Museen zu Berlin*, 4.1141. [23-25].

---

4. Finally, imperial slavery involved working in the household of the emperor. Some of these slaves held positions of power and wealth second only to the emperor himself.

Narcissus, the freedman of Emperor Claudius, amassed 400 million sesterces, one of the largest fortunes of the early empire. We know that even powerful senators treated Narcissus with respect. Imagine that! Claudius and other emperors used their imperial slaves to help them run the empire, trusting them more than the senators themselves.

In the Old Testament the word "servant" (*'ebed*) is sometimes used in regard to Israel's great heroes of the faith, thereby making it a designation of honor (1 Kings 8:53). Samuel describes how the Lord came to Nathan and said, "Go and tell my servant David" (2 Samuel 7:5). In a similar way God describes his prophets as "my servants" (Jeremiah 7:25).

Such passages demonstrate that in the Old Testament the term *servant* is often used in reference to those in positions of authority because they combine loyalty to God with humility before him. This is especially true of the "servant songs" of Isaiah 42-53. The Old Testament often describes people selected by God to bear authority as "servants." This designation indicates a humble willingness to be at God's disposal and to live according to his principles.

James may have meant something similar to what the early church intended when it used the Latin phrase *nolo episcopari* as the requirement for church office: "I do not wish to be a bishop." Only those who did not desire personal power could be trusted with authority within the church. The issue here is integrity and pure motives. James was a leader in the church because God placed him in that role, and he recognized and accepted it; he is not a leader because he desired power. James writes as one with authority, but also the mind of Christ, the servant of all.

We argued earlier that the word "slave" (*doulos*) needs to be understood not according to its contemporary English definition, but rather in light of the varieties of slave conditions within the Roman Empire. But we also argued that in this particular case there is insufficient evidence to conclude that James has only one particular image in mind.

We must remember that biblical writers thought in terms of concepts, to which any number of terms might fit. They did not usually think in terms of words with static meanings. The idea of the selfless love of God, for instance, is deeply lodged in Scripture. Writers such as C.S. Lewis have pointed out that this notion is linked to the Greek verb *agapao*. But as others have shown, the New Testament also uses the Greek verb *phileo* to express this idea, even though it is usually understood as expressing the concept of "brotherly love." These two words are often used interchangeably to convey the same idea.

In a similar manner, a single word or expression can imply varied meanings. Jesus, for example, fills the word *kyrios* ("Lord") with new meaning, so that in the New Testament it can imply either oppressor or servant-leader.

In short, biblical terms are far more flexible than we often allow.

James, as with Paul in Philippians 2, issues a strong call for servanthood as the central characteristic of the Christian life—modeled after Jesus himself. Indeed the Gospels present Jesus as a Servant-Messiah. At Jesus' baptism the voice from heaven combines kingship (Psalm 2) with service (Isaiah 42). The temptation accounts confirm that Jesus resolves to be a Servant-Messiah. Even Jesus' favorite self-designation, "Son of Man," points to this. While the Son of Man in Daniel 7 is to be served, Jesus attaches the idea of servanthood to the term: "The Son of Man did not come to be served, but to serve, and to give his life as a ransom for many" (Mark 10:45). He's the suffering servant of Isaiah 53 together with the Son of Man of Daniel 7.

Leaders in particular are to live out Jesus' model of servanthood. James makes this clear when in his opening greeting he combines images and themes of authority with comradeship and service. Church leadership ought to be reserved for those with no selfish agenda. Indeed, the church should be a place in which (in the proper contexts) we can be open and honest with each other, confident that we will receive encouragement, prayer, and even discipline when appropriate.

In verse 1 James describes himself as a "servant of God and of the Lord Jesus Christ." This is an odd wording, and it appears only here in the New Testament. These three names "Lord Jesus Christ" that make up the title refer to the unique character of Jesus. He is the exalted Lord who will one day return in glory. He is Jesus, God coming to earth in a human form. He is Christ, the anointed one who fulfilled God's purposes by dying for us.

Divine titles are linked elsewhere in James (1:27; 3:9). This wording in Latin (*dominus et deus*) meaning "Lord and God" was accepted by Emperor Domitian (AD 81-96), a development even the Romans found both extraordinary and unsettling. Romans were used to granting divine status only upon the death of the emperor.

Vespasian is famous for his sarcastic deathbed comment *Vae, puto deus fio* ("Alas, I think that I am becoming a god."). Vespasian grudgingly understood the need felt by the state to perpetuate the cult of emperor worship, but he harbored no illusions about his own status. Domitian, the son of Vespasian, however, took this address seriously, for he was a man of less ability, greater insecurity, and greater tyranny than his father.

Domitian was no friend of the early church, as he allowed fierce persecution. In Christian tradition he stands with Nero as a type of anti-Christ. Certainly his apparent claim of divine status reminded believers of the "man of lawlessness" in 2 Thessalonians 2.

The emperor's *apotheosis* (elevation to divine status) especially disturbed Jews and Christians, who believe God alone deserves such unwavering awe. Both groups were labeled "atheists" by the Romans because they believed in only one God, not the many gods of Mediterranean paganism. Perhaps

James used this word structure to designate the one who truly is Lord and God, countering the claims of the Roman state.

James' intent here also most likely demonstrates that loyalty to Jesus Christ does not undermine loyalty to God; that, in fact, they are one and the same (John 14:10). Balancing the divinity of Jesus Christ with monotheism was no small problem for early Christianity, and the formula James uses constitutes a portion of his answer to this dilemma.

The Romans believed that their conquests were laid upon them by fate—that they had a civilizing mission to exert on the rest of the world. They believed it was for the good of other peoples that they conquered. By some measures they were accurate—at times and in some places Rome could be a generous master.

> Three examples: (1) Under Emperor Trajan a policy was established whereby he lent money from his imperial treasury to Italian landowners, under the condition that they pay a 5 percent tax into a municipal chest, the revenue to be used to care for the children of needy families in that area. (2) In the correspondence between Trajan and Pliny, we read of the concern of Trajan for mundane matters, such as a proper water supply for provincial municipalities. (3) Emperor Tiberius, when given the advice to raise taxes in the provinces, replied that it is the part of a good shepherd to shear the flock, not skin it.
>
> —Suetonius, *Tiberius*, 32.

But the vast majority of those living under Roman rule did not have these experiences. They mostly knew the authority figures, rulers, and masters, whether Romans or provincial elites, only as oppressors.

Josephus tells us that the combination of Roman taxes and the temple tax "bled the country dry" (see his *Antiquities*, 17.304-8). Jewish farmers whose families were murdered by the Romans because they could not afford to pay their taxes turned to banditry and open rebellion because of the blunt edge of Roman rule.

Similarly, most slaves experienced their relationships with authority figures as less than desirable. Nor was the condition of urban household slavery a guarantee of well-being. Pliny, a first-century author, tells us that some were severely mistreated. In fact, the vast bulk of the population—women and men, slaves, peasants, and poor urbanites who together composed more than 90 percent of the population—perceived authority as generally callous, indifferent, and demeaning. Much of our world believes similarly. We experience authority negatively and as primarily self-interested.

James here paints a different picture, however. In his world and ours the combination of authority with service, which he conveys by use of the term *doulos*, is rare. Our familiarity with the idea and the phrase "servant leadership" may have jaded us. But Jesus calls us to live it out, not merely to pay it lip service.

The kingdom of God has upside-down priorities. The wisdom of God is foolishness to the world, and the wisdom of the world is foolishness to God. Leadership—especially leadership in the church—is to be undertaken only in concert with a commitment to seek God's will and others' well-being.

The identification of Jesus Christ as Lord was a radical statement in James's time. To the Jews it was blasphemous because no human could be called "Lord," and to the Romans it was treason against the authority of the emperor. To everyone who claimed it, it was a sign of giving Christ control over life, career, and ultimately destiny. Thousands of believers eventually lost their lives in horrible ways because they would not take back their statement: "Jesus is Lord."

—*Life Application Bible Commentary: James*, 3.

James 1:1b

¹ᵇTo the twelve tribes scattered among the nations:

Greetings.

James' addressees are "the twelve tribes scattered among the nations." This expression is also unusual. The only parallel in the New Testament is found in 1 Peter 1:1 where the addressees seem to be Gentile Christians who are "foreigners and exiles" (1 Peter 2:11).

Given the original 12 tribes of Israel no longer existed in James' time, there are at least two main lines of interpretation for the meaning he's after:

1. The "twelve tribes" refers to all Jews including or not including Jewish Christians living outside Palestine;
2. The expression is more symbolic of diverse Christians around the world.

Some point out that the original meaning of "the twelve tribes" was restricted to ethnic Israel. This argument suggests that when we uncover the original meaning of a term, we uncover its meaning in a text; this is called the "etymological argument." It's widely held as a sure route to truth, but it's often false.

We should not be swayed uncritically by the siren song of original meaning. While discovering the original meaning of a term may be satisfying and ultimately helpful, that's no guarantee we've discerned the meaning the author intended.

For example in the Old Testament the term *ger* ("stranger") was originally used as a self-reference by the Patriarchs (Genesis 21:23; 23:4), because they wandered in a foreign land. Even the name Moses gave to his son, Gershom, reflects this idea. Once firmly established in the land, however, *ger* came to refer to non-Jews. The point is that a term means exactly what the author wishes it to mean, neither more nor less.

In summary, James writes with the knowledge that he's been given authority in the church—but that this authority also means *service*: Service to God and service to others. James addresses his letter to the multiracial church scattered throughout the earth and the multiform Judaism (Pharisees, Sadducees, Essenes, Zealots, Christians) of the first century. The people addressed in this letter have been scattered and displaced as a result of persecution (Acts 11:19). These people must have felt unsettled and disheartened; many were homeless and marginalized. They must have had difficult lives.

Finally, James writes with sensitivity regarding Jewish monotheism but desires to make the case that loyalty is due to Jesus Christ, and that this loyalty does not endanger loyalty to God. Further James emphasizes that loyalty to Jesus and loyalty to God amount to the same thing.

This idea also carries with it an implied warning today: Loyalty to the government, to a particular political party or philosophy, to a particular religious expression, or to anything else besides God and the related commitment to be humble before God always contains the potential for the seeds of idolatry to germinate and flourish.

Many in the evangelical community identify the United States with Christianity. While the United States can at times stand for what is moral and right, often it does not. To confuse loyalty to the state with loyalty to God is idolatry—the same idolatry to which the ancient Israelites fell prey. James here pushes us to consider the ways we unwisely grant loyalty elsewhere that rightfully pertains to God alone.

James closes the opening words of his letter with the usual practice in Greek to employ the term *chairein* ("greetings" conveys a sense of joy or happiness). The typical form in Hebrew was *shalom* ("peace"), although among Greek-speaking Jews *chairein* was common. Today we would use the English word "hello."

READ BETWEEN THE LINES

- What do I know about the life of James?
- What would it be like having Jesus as an older brother?
- Why doesn't James brag a little about who he is?
- What does it mean to be a servant? A *slave*? Compare the meaning of these words from the first century and today.
- What does the term "Lord Jesus Christ" mean?
- Who are the "twelve tribes scattered among the nations"?
- Why the salutation "Greetings"?
- How can words have more than one meaning?

WELCOME TO MY WORLD

- Would I rather receive a letter, an email, a text message, or a Tweet from a friend? Why?
- James described himself in his opening; how would I describe myself?
- Who do I want to send a Christian letter to?
- Describe my feelings from a time when I had to move?
- Who do I serve?
- When I think of *slavery* today, what comes to mind?
- How may it appear at times that I desire power and authority?
- How does this balance with a sense of a "calling" in what I do?
- How does my life reflect humility?
- What does "servant leadership" mean to me in light of this passage?

- How does my church reflect being a multiracial church like that of the first century?
- Is there a difference between loyalty to God and loyalty to the state? Explain.

James follows his introduction and greeting with a passage containing practical questions and answers rich in theological content. In James 1:2-8 he addresses the question of trials: What is the source of misfortune? Why does God allow difficulties in our lives? How are we to respond to them? These are real-world questions. Who hasn't asked them? To these questions James answers that prayer, and specifically the wisdom of God, are the tools necessary to negotiate successfully the minefield of trials and the questions they spur in our minds.

Trials and Temptations

James 1:2

²Consider it pure joy, my brothers and sisters, whenever you face trials of many kinds,

James 1:2-6 is the rest of a chain "argument" by the use of verbal links: the words "greetings" (*chairein*) and "joy" (*charan*) in verses 1 and 2; "perseverance" in verses 3 and 4; "lack" in verses 4 and 5; "ask" in verses 5 and 6. James makes his case in James 1:2-8 that testing ought to be received with joy, for it is beneficial and that wisdom is needed as the gift from God in order to perceive testing in this manner.

James tells us to "consider" (i.e., count, evaluate) trials as pure joy. Warren W. Wiersbe points out that this is a financial term. When the apostle Paul became a Christian (Acts 9:1-19) he considered his life and set new goals and priorities (Philippians 3:7-11). In other words, things that were important became worthless in the light of his experience with Christ. When we face the trials of life, we must consider them in the light of what God is doing for us.

To respond to difficulties with joy seems at first absurd. Most of us spend a lot of our time attempting to avoid trials. But James is not encouraging us to go through life with a false smile plastered on our faces, acting giddy in the midst of difficult and dangerous situations. James knows as does the writer of Hebrews (12:11a) that "No discipline seems pleasant at the time."

Then in verse 3 he offers his answer to our natural question: Why would we rejoice in the midst of trials? This pure joy is based on confidence in the outcome of the trial. This is seeing life from God's perspective.

Trials have a purifying quality: they are the arena in which something good develops. We have limited control over our environment and the things that happen to us, but we can control how we respond to them. Hebrews 12:11b goes on to tell us "…Later on, however, it produces a harvest of righteousness and peace for those who have been trained by it."

Even our Lord understood this joy in the midst of extreme suffering in Hebrews 12:2, "For the joy set before him he endured the cross, scorning its shame…" Paul writes in 2 Corinthians 7:4, "…in all our troubles my joy knows no bounds."

Joy is different than mere happiness (although at times joy may *produce* happiness) that is determined by circumstances. Joy is referring to being content in every situation. In the phrase "pure joy," *pure* is translated from the original Greek word *pasan* ("whole, complete"), which heightens the effect of joy. So the "joy" James speaks of here is a complete, overflowing joy.

In short, joy is a decision more than a feeling. It means *choosing* to live above the feelings while not denying them. Because trials can be joy-robbers if we lack the proper attitude.

> "Joy is the best makeup."
> —Anne Lamott, *Grace (Eventually): Thoughts on Faith*

With "my brothers and sisters" we revisit the question of addressees. Earlier we came to two conclusions: First, James speaks with authority, but as one among peers; second, James writes to the multiracial, scattered church. "My brothers and sisters" conveys warmth and comradeship. James writes to encourage his "brothers and sisters" in the faith. The good news is we're not in this life alone. We have God and each other.

This leaves the question of the ethnic identification of his "brothers and sisters." By far the most established use of the term was within the early church. Here "brothers and sisters" could be used of fellow Jews, as Paul sometimes did

(Romans 9:3), but the overwhelming use in the New Testament and early Christian literature is of fellow Christians.

The widespread use of "brothers and sisters" in the New Testament was the result of Jesus using the term (Matthew 23:8; Mark 3:35; Luke 22:32) and of the radically different definition he gave to community. Loyalty to God, not ethnic composition, was his definition.

James teaches that Christians sometimes "face" trials because of this loyalty to God. The Greek word used here (*peripipto*) suggests an unwelcome and unanticipated experience (e.g., we "encounter" or "fall into" trials). Jesus uses the same term when he tells the story of the good Samaritan, as the man "fell into the hands of" robbers (Luke 10:36). There is no room here for the idea some have of seeking out trials as a way of "proving" your faith to yourself or to others. The trials James refers to here burst into our lives and are unexpected and, at least initially, unwelcome.

The trials "of many kinds" probably arose from both external and internal sources. There is little doubt that a variety is in view; they are multicolored, intricate, and diverse. Trials come in many shapes and sizes (physical, emotional, mental, social, spiritual, and financial, to name a few). Notice James does not say, "...*if* you face trials of many kinds." James instead uses the word "whenever," indicating that distress, adversity, and challenges are on their way if they haven't already arrived. God tells us to expect trials.

My wife and I once visited a world-famous weaver and watched his men and women work on the looms. I noticed that the undersides of the rugs were not very beautiful; the patterns were obscure and the loose ends of yarn dangled. "Don't judge the worker or the work by looking at the wrong side," our guide told us. In the same way, we are looking at the wrong side of life; only

> the Lord sees the finished pattern. Let's not judge Him or His work from what we see today. His work is not finished yet!
>
> **—Warren W. Wiersbe, *Be Mature, James*, 32.**

Testing, however, can be linked to Satan. James does not mention Satan in this passage (he alludes to Satan throughout his letter but specifically in 3:6 and clearly in 4:7), yet in the rabbinic theology upon which James draws, Satan is viewed as one of the sources of evil and misfortune—a view Jesus shared. It's important for us briefly to discuss the biblical view of Satan.

In the Old Testament, Satan (from the Hebrew *satan*, meaning "to accuse" or "to oppose") seems to have a God-given appointment as the prosecuting attorney, a role he performs in Job 1-2 and Zechariah 3. While clearly interested in pursuing his own designs, he is still somewhat restrained to oppose God's authority. But in the New Testament, Satan is openly hostile to God and has gathered about himself minions, both natural and supernatural. In addition to his legal gown he has also appropriated to himself both the mantle of tyrant and the disguise of *agent provocateur*. He is the strong man who, without legal rights, has gained *de facto* control over the earth. When in the temptation narratives Satan offers Jesus all the kingdoms of the earth, he has the power, but not the right, to do so.

Satan provokes us to sin. His usual path is one of stealth and deceit (Genesis 3:1; 2 Corinthians 11:14), preying on our moral imperfections. He is especially successful when he masquerades as good. He operates chiefly through institutions and structures, the "principalities and powers." Rome is described in Revelation as the consort of the beast, as a tool in Satan's hands. The crucifixion severely curtailed Satan's power (John 12:31), but he is still dangerous.

Satan and God are viewed as in conflict and competition over human beings. In this view Satan hopes to lead people away from God and then to cause them to suffer. Paul, like James, is aware of these developments. In his view Satan has a part in leading people astray (2 Corinthians 2:11), and Paul knows of the evil impulse (Romans 7:13-23) and of its pure counterpart, the Holy Spirit (8:1-17).

There are also links to the Gospels. Popular Jewish belief held that misfortune could be the result of either some internal fault or drive or some external force. The first is well illustrated in John 9:1-2. When passing the temple, Jesus and his disciples notice a man born blind. In asking Jesus if the man or his parents sinned, the disciples express a popular belief that this man experienced misfortune as a result of sin. Both the New Testament and rabbinic tradition recognized that Satan can and does entice human beings to sin (the temptation of Jesus: Matthew 4:1-11; Luke 4:1-13).

But we must not view all trials necessarily as the tools of Satan. Many in the name of Christ claim that sickness and infirmity are signs of sin or satanic attack or both. The Bible makes it clear that sickness can be the result of sin or Satan. But the Bible also makes it clear that this is not always the case. God sometimes uses infirmity for his purpose (1:12-18), as with Paul's thorn in the flesh (2 Corinthians 12:7-10) or the man born blind (John 9:1-2).

Not all sickness or infirmity is an attack. We do a disservice to others when we teach this, as we load them with guilt. Trials can be a part of the normal ebb and flow of life. No matter their source, James insists that we should respond not with anger or disappointment, but with utter joy.

James 1:3

3because you know that the testing of your faith produces perseverance.

The word "testing" reminds us of 1 Peter 1:7 where Peter combines trials and gold. The gold prospector brings his ore sample into an assayer's office to be tested to see if it is truly gold. God's approval of our faith is priceless because it assures us that our faith is genuine.

The result of the testing of faith is it produces perseverance—a highly prized trait. The word "produces" reminds us of a harvest where the end is in sight but it can take time. "Perseverance" (*hupomone*) is a new feature added to the character of a Christian in the midst of testing. It means steadfastness, staying power, patience, constancy, fortitude, and a determination under adversity. In other words "don't quit." Perseverance also means trusting God for a long duration. As Charles Swindoll would say, we need "to hang in there." (For an opposite example, Abraham ran ahead of the Lord, married Hagar, and brought great sorrow into his home (Genesis 16). He did not "hang in there.")

Perseverance is colored with the idea of hope, which animates and enriches these other qualities. The focus is not necessarily on the trial but to look beyond the trial to its potential outcome. This is not just positive thinking but an inner confidence in trusting God through it all.

There is a temptation in youth ministry to step in and rescue students from difficult experiences in life.

A man found the cocoon of an emperor moth. He took it home so that he could watch the moth come out of its cocoon. One day a small opening appeared. He sat and watched the moth for several hours as the moth struggled to force its body through the little hole. Then it seemed to stop making any progress. It appeared as if it had gotten as far as it could and it could go no further. It just seemed to be stuck. The man, thinking he'd act kindly, decided to help the moth—so he took scissors and snipped off the remaining bit of cocoon. The moth then emerged easily.

But it had a swollen body and small, shriveled wings. The man continued to watch the moth because he expected that at any moment the wings would enlarge and expand to be able to support the body, which would contract in time.

Neither happened. In fact, the little moth spent the rest of his life crawling around with a swollen body and shriveled wings. It never was able to fly.

What the man in his "kindness" and impatience failed to grasp was that the restricting cocoon and the struggle required for the moth to squeeze through the tiny opening were God's pathway of forcing fluid from the moth's body into its wings so that it would be ready for flight once it achieved freedom from the cocoon.

Freedom and flight would only come after struggle. And by depriving the moth of struggle, the man deprived the moth not only of its health but also of its potential.

Sometimes trials and struggles are exactly what we need. If God removed all the obstacles in our lives all the time, we'd never grow.

Do you know how a pearl is formed in an oyster? The oyster gets a few grains of sand lodged inside of its shell. These grains of sand produce a wound that irritates the oyster endlessly. After several months of struggle the wound turns into a beautiful pearl. But, there is never a pearl without a wound.

James 1:4

4Let perseverance finish its work so that you may be mature and complete, not lacking anything.

"Perseverance" is also a means to an end. We should not be satisfied with reliability, as important as this virtue is, but we should let it grow to its fullest, in order to become mature and complete, not lacking anything (see also Romans 6:1-23 and Galatians 5:6).

"Mature" (*telios*) denotes a "goal" or "rightful purpose."

This is a key term for James; no New Testament book uses it more often. Maturity here is not age related; it refers to what we have learned from the trials of life. It implies that God is a part of whatever process is involved in the formation of character. It's not some unachievable high standard, either. Rather, we can become persons of integrity, single-minded in our loyalty and devotion to God.

The "complete" person is one whose character is fully formed according to Christian standards; it is not "perfection," according to some standard common to popular culture. Paul found many in the church in Corinth guilty of accepting the standards of their society, and he reminded them that the wisdom of God appears foolish to this world, just as the wisdom of this world is foolishness in the sight of God (1 Corinthians 1:18-31). God wants a finished "product" who is mature and complete.

We commonly think in terms of two categories: We are human; God is divine. Perhaps there are three categories. We speak of Jesus as both human (for example being thirsty and fatigued in John 4 or to his weeping at the grave of Lazarus in John 11) and divine.

When God created humankind, we were made in God's very image. But as a result of the Fall, we endure an existence that's less than God intended. In other words, subhuman. That is why Psalm 8, the first commentary on Genesis 1:26-27, can speak of humanity (as first created) as *just a little lower than the angels* because the psalmist speaks of human beings as God originally intended—in close, constant communion with him.

In James we find this tension—between who we are as fallen human beings and who God calls us to be. As human beings we are frail, we fail; therefore we need God's grace, care, and forgiveness. But we are called to become authentically human. God must work in us before he can work through us (look at the lives of Abraham, Moses, and Joseph).

Ours is not a religion of works, but it does involve a call to action. God—who gives this call to be like Christ—is also a God who forgives, for God understands our pain and our frailty.

Still, James calls us to perfection. But while "perfection" may remind many of us of unhappy childhood experiences, unable to earn the desperately desired praise of parents or authority figures, this is not the notion of perfection James has in view.

Kathleen Norris, in "Why the Psalms Scare Us," explains it this way: "I have lately realized that what went wrong for me in my Christian upbringing is centered in the belief that one had to be dressed up, both outwardly and inwardly, to meet God." That is why she so appreciates the Psalms, for they "demand engagement, they ask you to read them with your whole self...through all the moods and conditions of life, and while you may feel awful, you sing anyway. To your surprise, you find that the psalms do not deny your true feelings but allow you to reflect on them, right in front of God and everyone."

A friend told me about a Catholic priest who ministers to women who have had abortions. He tells them that abortion is a terrible sin, but an equally terrible sin is not allowing God to forgive you if you have had an abortion. God, he tells them, wants them to come to him, for God loves them deeply. Honesty before God does not keep us from God; rather, it allows us to know him and to be known by him. It is the first step on the path that leads to our union with him. It is a path marked by trials and prayer, and it leads to perfection.

James 1:5

⁵**If any of you lacks wisdom, you should ask God, who gives generously to all without finding fault, and it will be given to you.**

At this point James moves from moral integrity to wisdom (*sophia*), whose only source is God. The Old Testament has many references to God as the source of wisdom including Proverbs 2:6, "For the LORD gives wisdom, and from his mouth comes knowledge and understanding." While human beings are, at least in part, responsible for their moral development, wisdom comes only from God. In the New Testament generally, wisdom is allied to understanding God's purposes and plan and a determination to live accordingly.

We need wisdom to know how to cope with trials, for wisdom provides God's perspective. With wisdom we perceive misfortune as an opportunity for God to bring about his purpose. Wisdom, as the gift of God, logically leads to our asking for it. Here again we see verbal links to Jesus: "Ask and it will be given to you" (Matthew 7:7; Luke 11:9); "And I will do whatever you ask in my name, so that the Father may be glorified in the Son" (John 14:13).

In the Old Testament, wisdom can be searched out. In ancient Palestine and in our culture people associated wisdom with age and experience. But for James, wisdom is God's gift to Christians, granted as the result of prayer. In James wisdom has practical applications, as it results in a series of qualities (humility, perseverance, patience) that end up preserving community.

James also contrasts the wisdom of God with the wisdom of the world. Wisdom is not just knowledge (the accumulation of information). Heavenly wisdom helps us make sense of life's injustices and difficulties. However, even if we fail to understand, we still trust in God.

By contrast, the world's wisdom says to avoid trials and misfortunes. From this point of view it doesn't take much of a leap to conclude that trials are proof that God doesn't care about us or is unable to act on our behalf. James warns against these erroneous points of view in 1:12-16.

James goes on to say that God gives generously without hesitation, contrasting God's single-hearted devotion and purpose to the evil one's fraudulent schemes. God also gives "without finding fault" (*me oneidizontos*). The root word means "to utter insult" and carries an active tone. In other words, when we come to God in prayer asking for wisdom, God does not belittle us ("What, you again? Weren't you here five minutes ago? Gabriel get me the club."). Rather, God welcomes us with open arms and is pleased to give us the wisdom we need. But while God never hesitates to give to us, we sometimes hesitate to ask. Taken altogether, James conveys the notion that God's generosity is unwavering, regardless of our previous record (Luke 6:35).

Solomon in the Old Testament prayed for wisdom (1 Kings 3:9); but by asking for wisdom he already proved he was wise.

James 1:6-7

6But when you ask, you must believe and not doubt, because the one who doubts is like a wave of the sea, blown and tossed by the wind. 7That person should not expect to receive anything from the Lord.

James now turns his attention to those who don't receive wisdom from God. To them he says to ask God without doubt—that is, without waffling back and forth. He employs the metaphor of a rudderless vessel in the midst of a sea, buffeted by strong winds. This thought echoes Ephesians 4:13-14, where Paul speaks of our maturing as Christians, until we are no longer children tossed to and fro, carried about by every wind of doctrine. James not only explains *what* to ask for (wisdom), but also describes *how* to ask (in faith).

> Verse 6 offers the human side of prayer. Although Luther took a generally dim view of the letter of James, this verse he viewed with favor, as he wrote in his *Instructions for the Visitors of Parish Pastor*: "The Pastors should also instruct their people that prayer includes faith that God will hear us, as James writes in James 1."
>
> —*Luther's Works*, ed. Conrad Bergendoff (Philadelphia: Muhlenberg, 1958), 40:278-79.

Verse 6 conveys a difficult message, primarily due to the meaning and implications of the word "believe." Some suggest that effective prayer is carried out with confidence and in full conviction, especially with a belief that manifests itself in works. In contrast is the view that "belief" here means "confidence in prayer." It means coming to God, believing that God is able.

There are strong objections to this second view, however. James has just laid down the idea of the universal generosity of God, and it's unclear how this can be rectified with the image of God giving only to those with sufficient confidence that God can accomplish a certain task. Some argue, however, that it is precisely this confidence that unleashed the healing powers of Jesus. This is a misconception.

The common view that Jesus was unable to heal unless there was sufficient faith in the heart of the one afflicted is easily proven false. No one would argue that Lazarus (John 11:1-46), or the daughter of Jairus (Matthew 9:18-26; Mark 5:21-43; Luke 8:40-56), or even anyone in attendance at either of these occasions, had faith for an instant resurrection.

Of course there's Mark 6:1-5, in which we're told that in Nazareth Jesus "could not do any miracles there...[because of] their lack of faith." But careful inspection of the text reveals that Jesus *did* heal people of afflictions in Nazareth, surely what we would consider miracles. The point here is that miracles don't necessarily "cause" faith (see Luke 16:31); and so Jesus declines to perform them when he perceived that the result would be the *wrong kind* of belief—namely a belief in Jesus, the wonder-worker. This incorrect belief—perhaps a belief in their own vision of what the Messiah was to do and be—characterized the minds of the disciples who left Jesus in John 6:66. Jesus sought to create and nurture a different kind of belief—a belief in Jesus as God's agent, as the one who reveals the living God.

Those who hold this position also believe that the doubter has no such confidence that he or she will be healed. However, in Mark 9:14-32 Jesus heals a boy with an evil spirit. In verse 24 the father of the boy exclaims, "I do believe; help me overcome my unbelief!"

It is therefore more likely that James means a faith that manifests itself in action. Further, in James 2:22, James describes the faith of Abraham as one of faith and actions working together. So perhaps James is arguing that those who are growing in the will of the Father will receive even more room for grace. This is essentially the thought in John 14:13-14.

The contrast here is with "doubt," and since doubt is a waffling back and forth, the result of doubt is inaction. The one who doubts vacillates and is tossed to and fro as on a tempestuous sea. But it's not honest, intellectual doubts in question here; after all, to doubt is human, as the Psalms insist. David himself gives voice to his doubts about the character and trustworthiness of God. In Psalm 6 he wonders aloud if God has rejected him, and he even attempts to force God into action by an obvious bribe. Yet in the midst of this honest doubt, David is reminded of all that God has done for him in the past, and he gains the hope necessary to continue.

James 1:8

8Such a person is double-minded and unstable in all they do.

Faith here is from one who understands and has experienced the character of God—the God who gives freely and generously. Because of this experience we can have confidence. A prayer should be offered in integrity; it should be single-hearted, even as God has integrity and is single-hearted.

James describes the one who doubts as double-minded (*dipsychos*) or having a divided mind. Behind this stands the Hebrew idea of being double-tongued or double-faced (Psalm 11:2). Deuteronomy 26:16 warns the Israelites against worshiping God with two hearts; also Psalm 12:2 speaks of this double heart. Such a heart contrasts sharply with God, who is single-hearted. James is speaking of someone who constantly changes allegiances and cultivates the outer surface layer of faith, wrongly thinking robotic action to be the heart of faith. James calls us to be people of character, whose faith manifests itself in action in accord with who God has called each one of us to be.

James touches upon an important biblical theme here: *God is the one who means what he says, who always accomplishes his purpose*: "So is my word that goes out from my mouth: It will not return to me empty, but will accomplish what I desire and achieve the purpose for which I sent it" (Isaiah 55:11). God's word is like a hammer that splinters rock (Jeremiah 23:29). The words of human beings, by contrast, are often *only wind* (Job 16:3); they *cannot stand up* (Isaiah 8:10); and they *fall to the ground* (1 Samuel 3:19).

James has in mind not only a simple confidence that God can answer our cries, but also has added a deeper commitment to live in the will of the Father—even if that aspiration is one at which we often fail. What is clearly excluded is the person for whom faith is a matter of little or no account, whose words are not in line with the heart.

Double-minded people are "unstable in all they do." This phrase denotes those who're unsettled, not at rest. Being "unstable" is the quality that marks one's whole existence, not just spiritual life. It carries the idea of inclining this way and that, but never fully committing. This word is rare in Greek literature before James, but prevalent in Christian literature afterward, which perhaps speaks to James' influence.

Modern Christians often think of doubt as something to be avoided. The Bible however knows the healthy and even helpful effects of honest doubt. The doubt James wants us to avoid is not honest doubt, but doubt that leads to temptation.

Human beings, according to James, experience a full range of emotions, including doubt, anger, and pain. In this James has much in common with the Psalms that deal honestly with human emotion. Sometimes the psalmist expresses anger at other human beings, and perhaps even at God, as it seems as if the Lord has allowed the wicked to flourish, even though the psalmist has tried to rein in his emotions and his tongue (Psalm 35:17; 39:1-3;).

In the press of life we, like the psalmist, often wonder where God is, whether God really cares, and why God waits: the pain of a couple mourning the death of an 11-month-old daughter; a family grieving over a 19-year-old woman killed on her way to church by a drunk driver. Such people know the pain of random, senseless loss. They know what it's like to cry out to God in despair and even in doubt.

But honest doubt drives us to remember all that God has done in the past—and therefore to remember the steadfast, trustworthy character of God (Psalm 77:7-12). While at times our lives offer sorrow so profound that we question God, ultimately we know his character and his touch of compassion. God knows us and meets us in the frailty, weakness, and dirtiness of the human condition. To pretend that our lives are otherwise is to lie to ourselves and to God. Like David we must say to God, "My sin is always before me" (Psalm 51:3). We can do it with joy and confidence because we know the character of God, who has proven himself to be a God who forgives, who can turn sin into something good, who can turn weeping into joy.

READ BETWEEN THE LINES

- What is pure joy?
- Why does he call his audience "brothers and sisters"?
- What are the trials James is referring to?
- What is the source of misfortune?
- How has my faith been tested?
- What is faith?
- How would I define perseverance?
- What is the work "perseverance" is finishing?
- How would I define being "mature and complete"?
- Define wisdom.
- Who am I to go to in order to receive wisdom?
- What does it mean to "give generously"?
- What does "without finding fault" mean?
- What does it mean to "believe" with "no doubt"?
- How is doubt like a wave of the sea?
- What are the characteristics of a double-minded person?
- How are the readers of James' letter unstable?

WELCOME TO MY WORLD

- Why is my life so hard?
- What is one of the greatest trials I have faced so far in my life?
- What is the greatest trial I'm facing now?

- Describe a challenging experience that increased my perseverance.
- What difference does my faith make?
- When have I been tempted to quit?
- What do I think God would say to someone about to bail out of the faith in the midst of a trial?
- How do I usually respond when I face a trial?
- Who do I usually turn to in the midst of trials?
- How can I prepare for trials?
- When I feel like giving up what do I do?
- What pain is the most difficult to bear (physical, mental, social, emotional)?
- How am I to respond to misfortune and difficulties?
- Why did God let this (trial/test/misfortune) happen to me?
- How should I pray when I face a trial?
- How can I rejoice in the midst of my trials?
- What difference does faith make in my life?
- Where am I on a "maturity" scale of 1-10?
- In a trial what should I pray and how should I pray?
- Describe a time when I doubted.
- What will I do now after reading this section of James when a trial comes upon me?

Poverty and Wealth

James 1:9-11

⁹Believers in humble circumstances ought to take pride in their high position. ¹⁰But the rich should take pride in their humiliation—since they will pass away like a wild flower. ¹¹For the sun rises with scorching heat and withers the plant; its blossom falls and its beauty is destroyed. In the same way, the rich will fade away even while they go about their business.

James now turns to the questions of poverty and wealth within the Christian community. James uses two paradoxes in this passage. Webster defines a *paradox* as "a statement that is seemingly contradictory or opposed to common sense and yet is perhaps true." The first is the paradox of the "poor rich" and the second is the paradox of the "rich poor."

The excesses of Solomon and his successors led the prophets to castigate the bloated rich for their lack of concern for the poor. In a similar fashion, the priestly aristocracy of the second temple period (530 BC to AD 70, when the *Second Temple* of Jerusalem existed) was known for its material excesses.

This led to two popular conclusions:

1. The poor were the devoutly religious, for they had supported Judas Maccabeus (acclaimed as one of the greatest warriors in Jewish history alongside Joshua, Gideon, and David) who led the Maccabean revolt in 167–160 BC against the Hellenizing aristocracy in Jerusalem.
2. Wealth tends to make its possessor double-minded (just as, in the view of the poor, the priestly aristocracy had sold out their religion and people in the interests of personal power).

James is intent upon playing off these two popular views in verses 9 and 10. Verse 9 stops you in your tracks, as it seems to appear suddenly and has little to do with what has come before. But upon further reflection the connections come into focus:

1. The conditions of poverty constitute another "trial," parallel to others already described by James.
2. The contrast between faith and double-mindedness seems to parallel that between humility and wealth.

The word translated "humble" is *tapeinos*, meaning insignificant in the world's eyes, lowly, relatively poor and powerless, lacking in material possessions. Jesus said, "Happy are those who realize that they are spiritually poor." As Cyprian Norwid said, "To be what is called happy, one should have something to live on, something to live for, and something to die for."

Are both the poor and the rich...*Christian*? All agree that the poor brother is a member of the Christian community—but what about the rich man? There are abundant reasons for viewing the rich man as a Christian. Grammatically, the term "believers" and the phrase "take pride in" found in verse 9 are linked to "rich" in verse 10. Furthermore, to suppose that the rich are *not* members of the Christian community seems strange. For if they're outside of it, why should they even think about living according to Christian principles?

Many commentators opt to believe that the rich person is not a member of the Christian community. These scholars point out that the word *plousios* ("rich") is used in 2:7 exclusively of non-Christians. This means that "take pride in" here must be ironic: In other words, the rich have had their day, and all they can look forward to is the judgment after death. This line of interpretation, it is claimed, complements James' teaching that the poor will be vindicated but the rich destroyed.

But there is another way to understand the matter: The wealthy whom Amos dubbed "cows of Bashan" (Amos 4:1-3) were Israelites, and yet they received condemnation, because their actions were not in line with their claim to be children of Abraham. Like the cows of Bashan it is possible that the "rich" in James includes wealthy members of the Christian community whose life patterns yield little or no evidence of Christian commitment, thereby disqualifying them from true membership. This is not a matter of "eternal security." Rather, the idea here is in line with the words of John the Baptist (Matthew 3:9) that God could take rocks and make children of Abraham out of them. The question is one of loyalty manifesting itself in action.

This is one of the issues in 1 Corinthians 11, describing rich Christians, in copying the Roman public feasts, sponsored a Eucharist marked by social and economic status. Roman feasts always separated the rich and poor; now Christians were importing Roman cultural values into church practices—values that elevated status and wealth as worth determiners in the community's eyes. Paul responded with disappointment.

The humble should rejoice because their poverty provides an arena for their faith to be tested and thus for endurance to grow, and they will be exalted, just as the prophets and Jesus had promised. These poor are poor both spiritually and materially. The ancient world knew almost nothing of what we would call a "middle class." About 90 percent of the population of the Roman Empire lived at or below what people today would consider the poverty level. Except in select urban locations such as Corinth, social climbing in the Roman world was a virtual impossibility. But they are also poor spiritually, and here James taps into the rich theology of the poor in Judaism, where poverty and righteousness go hand in hand.

Poverty, James says, can be a place for trials in and through which our character can be shaped and molded. There is a rich theological heritage within Judaism linking poverty with spirituality, for the poor feel most keenly the universal human need for God.

In verse 10 the rich, like their riches, don't last. They will pass away and wither in the scorching heat of the summer wind. James' "scorching heat" reminds me of my many years living in the arid climate of Southern California. I vividly remember the "Santa Anas." Those hot rushing winds come off the desert for several days at a time. The heat blows off the desert similar to the wave of heat that comes as an oven door is opened. The ground becomes so hot you can't walk barefoot on it. Lawns and shrubs can be destroyed in a few days if left unattended. Plants must be watered each evening.

The image is meant to convey both the suddenness of this unease and the frailty of much we deem secure. This is the lot of the rich, James writes, who refuse to see the world from God's perspective—rather their wealth plays the role of God.

James here calls upon us to think deeply about the foundation of our lives. We're all self-reliant to certain extents: on our money, our families, our talents. It takes a long time for God to teach us that our only hope when it comes down to it is God's trustworthiness. It can take a lifetime to learn this lesson, and James wants to remind us of the truth of this lesson.

Riches have the capacity to dull our sight until we fail to see the image of God in those around us. They have the potential to woo us into an uncritical acceptance of the standards of the world as the rightful standards of the church. Therefore the rich man should glory in his belittlement, not only because riches are transitory, but because they are a hindrance. Trials will either relieve him of this hindrance or force a shock of clarity. Trials, if properly understood through the gift of God's wisdom, will grant a new perspective in which riches are seen for what they are.

Indeed ours is a culture that places great value on what we think we deserve and upon what we want. Commercials suggest that what we want we deserve. Even commercials for Christian groups use this ploy. The Christian gospel tells us that all of us are afflicted by an inherent self-interest, the siren song of the *yetzer ha-ra*. Jesus calls us to deny ourselves (Deny yourself, take up your cross daily, and follow me.). We cannot deny what we do not recognize, and so James implores us to recognize this basic self-interest. It is the disease that afflicts each of us, and which the gospel claims we must deny.

The rich clinging to their wealth reminded me of monkeys.

I was told as a kid that monkeys are greedy and self-centered. I also remember hearing stories about how monkeys in other countries are captured. Holes the size of a monkey's hand were drilled in the tops of several coconuts. The coconuts would be drained of liquid and replaced with food monkeys liked. The altered coconuts were placed around the trees monkeys occupied. The monkeys came down, put their hands in the coconuts, and grabbed handfuls of food.

When the monkey "catchers" appeared from the bush, the monkeys fled—still holding the food inside their clenched fists... and the coconuts as well! The monkeys, wanting the food more than anything else, couldn't shake the coconuts because their fists were too big to get through the holes. This made them easy to catch because the monkeys couldn't climb trees wearing their newfound coconut "gloves."

—Les

James should not be construed here as advocating a nonchalant attitude toward the poor on the part of the wealthy, supposing that this status is somehow "good" for them. Nor does the passage allow for a pessimistic resignation to that status. James—and indeed the entirety of the New Testament—calls for community obligation. Christians who have the ability should put forth a responsible effort, in the interests of the greater good, to help the poor (2 Thessalonians 3:6-14). No matter what the situation, those with resources are called upon to use them wisely and generously.

James lived among and wrote to persons who knew poverty and hardship unimaginable to most of us. We mustn't emphasize the spiritual element here so that James' practical concerns are lost. We must let these ideas speak for themselves and then use them as a mirror for our own situations. All that we have—our health, our education, our wealth—are gifts from God. We have a *sacred* responsibility to use them wisely. The acclaimed University of California sociologist Robert Bellah says that what's missing in our culture is a sense of *connectedness*—to each other and to some greater cause.

READ BETWEEN THE LINES

- What are the poor to take pride in? Why?
- Are both the poor and the rich...*Christians*?
- Is this poverty described in James economic or spiritual?
- How are poverty and spirituality linked?
- Why should both groups "take pride"?
- What will happen to the rich and their riches?
- How is a wealthy person similar to a plant in the scorching heat?

WELCOME TO MY WORLD

- How do I copy the culture I live in?
- The world today and the Roman culture placed high

value on the markers of status and wealth. What about me?

- How do I determine a person's value?
- In the eyes of the rest of the world, would I be seen as rich?
- What am I doing with my money?
- Do I treat people of status and wealth differently than those of lesser status and poverty?

The Crown of Life

James 1:12

¹²Blessed is the one who perseveres under trial because, having stood the test, that person will receive the crown of life that the Lord has promised to those who love him.

Tragedy is often random and mindless: An infant is killed by a stray bullet fired in a drive-by shooting; an airliner crashes, killing hundreds; a young woman dies in an automobile accident, the victim of a drunk driver. Senseless tragedy leaves us feeling numb, powerless, and uncertain. James now turns his attention from those who endure and pass the test to those who need encouragement to hang in there before they abandon the effort.

Some see this verse as belonging with the previous passage, and indeed it serves as a bridge between 1:1-11 and 1:13-18. But because James provides what many believe is the second element of a double letter opening (the first being 1:2), the break should be here. The letter begins with an introduction (1:1), followed by the initial opening of the letter in which James presents the themes of trials, wisdom, and wealth (1:2-11). This second opening revisits and expands these themes, but it begins with the ideas of blessing and the crown of life.

James has pressed into service a standard theological point of Judaism—the idea that people faithful to God are called "blessed." In the Prophets (Isaiah 30:18; 56:2) and the wisdom tradition (Job 5:17; Psalm 32:1; 41:1; 94:12), many are called "blessed," including: those who seek God's forgiveness and those who do justice. James reminds his readers of these theological principles and uses them as a springboard for his new line of thought in verses 13-18—for these verses describe God's gracious giving and forgiving nature, the nature and purpose of trials, and the formation of godly character.

It seems clear that the Psalms, and more broadly the wisdom tradition, comprise important elements of the background fabric to James. This is not to say that James *is* an example of wisdom literature, however, as older commentaries often maintain. As in the wisdom tradition, the word "blessed" has both present and future connotations. Jesus used the word in each of what we call the Beatitudes (Matthew 5:3-12).

In using the word "blessed" (*makarios*) to describe Christians who endure, James is saying that Christians *belong* to God, for God has adopted us. We are a part of God's family and life. And like true children, we are to reflect our Father. Luke 6:35-36 records Jesus saying that if we are merciful as God is merciful, we will be called "children of the Most High."

Part of the meaning of blessing is tied to our being "mature and complete" (1:4), which is a foretaste of our reward, fully realized in the age to come. This idea includes intimacy with God and participation with God in accomplishing God's purpose. This is why so much of James is devoted to the practical components of living the Christian life. To become God's agent is to live in communion with God and to be about God's purpose. James isn't saying that the sinner is saved by enduring trials; rather that the believer is rewarded by enduring trials.

The one who perseveres is qualified to be called "blessed," and the reward is the "crown (*stephanos*) of life" (Psalm 8:5; 1 Peter 5:4; Revelation 2:10). In the Bible and in ancient Mediterranean culture, a "crown" was usually understood as the victor's crown (a wreath granted to victors at Olympus comes to mind) or an ornament of honor (Proverbs 1:9) or the royal crown or the crown of flowers worn on festive occasions such as weddings. In the Bible the first three types of crowns convey the ideas of reward and honor. In 1 Corinthians 9:24-25 Paul speaks of the crown as eternal life, which he compares to the perishable crown worn by victors at the games (2 Timothy 4:8; 1 Peter 5:4). In Philippians 4:1 he speaks of believers as his "joy and crown."

For James wisdom is needed to understand trials properly and also to gain the "crown of life." James does not imply a competition that eliminates all but the victor. For example, Paul in 1 Corinthians 9:24-25 contrasts the games in which only one can win to the life of spiritual endeavor, in which all can prove victorious. James indicates the crown is the mark of honor and the behavior that leads to eternal life. That is, the "crown of life" is eternal life, and in this age it is a life lived in the will of God as his faithful and loyal servant.

James then adds that this crown of life is what "the Lord has promised to those who love him." As his children, Christians are to stand fast, as do all who truly love God, in order to receive our inheritance. Here the theme of loyalty to God and of turning from lesser—and therefore potentially dangerous and false—loyalties is present. The faithful are those who stand the test, for real love for God manifests itself in action. James is here faithfully following the teaching of Jesus (Matthew 25:31-46).

A potential misstep has to do with the idea of reward as an inducement for faith and behavior. Particularly in the Protestant tradition we are most comfortable with "salvation as a free gift." To us the idea of a reward for living the Christian life seems distastefully like a bribe offered by God.

But we must distance ourselves from our modern idea of "bribe" and recognize that the New Testament is comfortable with its idea of reward. In 1 Corinthians 9:24-27 Paul employs the metaphor of a race to illustrate the Christian life, and he concludes with a startling statement: "I strike a blow to my body and make it my slave so that after I have preached to others, I myself will not be disqualified for the prize." In Philippians 3:14 he speaks of pressing on to the goal and prize for which God has called him heavenward in Christ Jesus. Even Jesus spoke of reward: "Rejoice and be glad, because great is your reward in heaven, for in the same way they persecuted the prophets who were before you" (Matthew 5:12). The New Testament idea of reward is not similar to our notion of a bribe. Rather it's a reminder of the dignity, gravity, and integrity of the calling of God to which we have responded—an appeal to our pure inclination and a reminder of the example of the saints who have gone before.

READ BETWEEN THE LINES

- What does it mean to be "blessed"?
- What are the characteristics of someone who perseveres?
- What's "the test"?
- What is the "crown of life"?
- Who gets the crown?
- How is this different from a bribe?
- What does it mean to love the Lord?

WELCOME TO MY WORLD

- Describe a reward I have received for persevering.
- Would I describe myself as blessed? Why?
- How does my life reflect that I love the Lord?

Temptations and Their Source

James 1:13

13When tempted, no one should say, "God is tempting me." For God cannot be tempted by evil, nor does he tempt anyone;

When misfortune strikes, we tend to look for something or someone to blame. It's common for humans to attribute difficulties or evil to Satan, or to God, or to the whims of fate.

Homer has Zeus complain: "It is incredible how easily human beings blame the gods and believe us to be the source of their troubles, when it is their own wickedness and stupidity that brings upon them sorrows more severe than any which Destiny would assign."

Proverbs 19:3 makes the point well: "A person's own folly leads to their ruin, yet their heart rages against the LORD." When confronted by God in the Garden of Eden, Adam pleads innocence and blames Eve (Genesis 3:12-13). Eve in turn blames the serpent, and by extension God the Creator. Neither takes responsibility for his or her actions. How human they are—and how quickly they prove themselves willing to place in jeopardy their relationship to each other and to God in the name of self-interest.

To this James offers a scathing response: "When tempted, no one should say, 'God is tempting me.'" James offers two reasons for this. God cannot be tempted by evil, nor does God tempt anyone. God never tempts his people; God never entices them to commit an evil act. God isn't even indirectly involved.

Further, when we accuse God or want God to prove himself, we're guilty of trying to tempt God. It's likely that James was reminded of the temptation narratives (Matthew 4:7; Luke

4:12) in which Jesus quoted Deuteronomy 6:16 in response to Satan: "Do not put the Lord your God to the test."

James knows the origin of temptation. It is not God, nor is it Satan alone. James makes his case that individuals are accountable, and that it's wrong to see difficult circumstances as the result of a God who can do evil or wishes to do good but does not have the power to aid those in distress. Temptation originates from a personal desire born of self-interest—and in that state renders us susceptible to the tricks of the evil one. We may wrongly blame others, but ultimately we are morally responsible.

The key term here is *epithymia*, which is translated "desire." There are normal desires of life given to us by God. If we did not feel hunger or thirst we would never eat or drink. Without fatigue, the body would never rest. Sex is a normal desire; without it the human race would not continue. However, in the New Testament *epithymia* generally carries a negative meaning, such as "lust," "selfish ambition," or "evil desire."

Unlike the case in James 1:2-8, here *peirasmos* ("temptation, trial") is clearly restricted to our hearts. There is a possibility of making a false step in interpreting the differences between "trial" and "temptation," since the same Greek word (*peirasmos*) means both. A "trial" to one person may well be the arena of "temptation" for another. In 1:2-12 the NIV renders *peirasmos* with the English word "trial." This word group occurs in 1:13 three times as a verb and once as an adverb; here the NIV translates *peirasmos* as "temptation." This change is not the result of convenient whim on the part of the translators of the NIV. James himself makes the distinction. In 1:2-11 "trials" are something to be endured, whereas in 1:13-14 "temptations" are something to be avoided. This is an example of polysemy, or multiple meanings of terms.

Here again the flexibility of the New Testament authors in the matter of words and their meanings is in evidence. We should be familiar with this phenomenon. In English, the word "sanction" bears two meanings that are opposed to each other. "Sanction" can mean "to approve," as in, "The professor gave her sanction for a group project to aid refugee children." But it can also intend disapproval, usually by way of penalty, as in, "Trade sanctions were leveled against them." With respect to James 1, particular "trials" or "temptations" may have different origins, but to human eyes, difficulties, no matter their origin, are troublesome. We tend to lay stress on the intent of the tempter: "He was tempting me." The New Testament lays stress on our reaction. If we give in, then the situation becomes a temptation. If we resist and persevere, then the situation is for us a trial that makes us stronger.

James emphasizes that God is not actively involved in the sending of temptation; in fact, God never tempts anyone. What makes the "test" a "temptation" is not that God has put us in such a position, but rather that we willingly disobey God. When circumstances are difficult we may begin complaining against God, questioning his love, and resisting his will. It takes spiritual discernment to see in difficulties the possibility of growth.

James 1:14

¹⁴but each person is tempted when they are dragged away by their own evil desire and enticed.

According to James, we are "dragged away" and "enticed" by evil desire (the promptings of the *yeser-ha-ra*). These expressions have their home in the realms of hunting and fishing. The fact that they appear in an odd order ("dragged away" is placed before "enticed") is best explained by the tendency of the Old Testament to mesh images of snares and nets. So in Ecclesiastes 9:12 we read, "As fish are caught in a cruel net, or birds taken in a snare, so people are trapped by evil times that fall unexpectedly upon them."

In other words, this verse contains two similar images, not a succession of action within one image. The first pictures the violent action of capture that follows setting a lure, and the second, the attractive bait that draws an unsuspecting victim. The extraordinary vividness of these images shows how dangerous James believes the evil impulse to be. Evil desire within us acts as both the attractive bait and as the lure. The evil desire is our own, and a decision to be attracted to it is equally our own responsibility. This deep character inclination explains the actions of the double-minded person in 1:6-8 and the wealthy person in 1:10. Jeremiah 17:9 tells us, "The heart is deceitful above all things and beyond cure. Who can understand it?"

Each of us has our own huge if-only list. If only I hadn't met her, if only I had gone to a different school, if only my parents weren't so strict, if only my parents didn't give me so much freedom, if only I didn't hang out with those kids, if only he didn't put that idea in my mind, if only...

A textbook example of this object of temptation and the internal lust is King David in 2 Samuel 11 and his encounter with Bathsheba. It began with a quick glance from his rooftop of her bathing and quickly progressed to sleeping with her while knowing she was the wife of Uriah. His sin did not end in adultery. To cover up his sin, David had Uriah killed. This happened to "a man after (God's) own heart" (1 Samuel 13:14). As Swindoll has said, "If such a great man of God can fall so suddenly, and so severely, we shouldn't think for a moment that it can't happen to us."

While James does not offer a full-blown theodicy (an attempt to reconcile the presence of evil with the belief in a good God), it is not unlikely that he has in mind the theology of the book of Job. When tragedy strikes, it is natural for us to inquire of God, but we should not allow this natural desire to grow into sin. In the depths of his despair, for example, Job said, "Though he slay me, yet will I hope in him" (Job 13:15). Here is combined the very human tendency to cry out to God, but it is a cry in the context of trust. In 1 Corinthians 10:13 Paul writes, "No temptation has overtaken you except what is common to mankind. And God is faithful; he will not let you be tempted beyond what you can bear. But when you are tempted, he will also provide a way out so that you can endure it."

James 1:15

15Then, after desire has conceived, it gives birth to sin; and sin, when it is full-grown, gives birth to death.

James' image of a lure that tempts and entices us to fall from the truth has many faces: stealing, lying, gossiping, cheating, envying, striving for popularity, vying for power—the list goes on. We will discuss two such lures, each of which is manifest in potent and varied ways in contemporary culture.

Because of the ability of sin to mask itself, a lure may appear harmless and innocent to our eyes, but in reality it has dire consequences. Take, for example, the powerful lure of success, especially if we can dress it in spiritual clothing.

Certainly, we think, if God is in this enterprise, then we will be successful. The members of the "prosperity" wing of American Protestantism would, of course, agree. However, sometimes God calls people to labor in vain, in fields that to our eyes appear barren. To such fields, for example, God called Jeremiah. Our definition of "the good" is not necessarily God's definition.

Success and acclaim easily crowd out the servant model the Bible places before us. This is one of the oldest of sins—the sin of pride. The fact that it is well known and yet continues to claim many victims is a testimony to the power and tenacity of sin and to the success of the hidden lure.

Like a snowball rolling downhill, sin grows more destructive the more we let it have its way. Thomas á Kempis has written, "At first [temptation] is a mere thought confronting the mind; then imagination paints it in stronger colors; only after that do we take pleasure in it, and the will makes a false move, and we give our assent."

The second lure dangled before us is the belief that sin isn't really sin, therefore we needn't take it seriously. Like Paul we need to see that there is something irrational about our behaviors in light of our commitments: "I do not understand what I do. For what I want to do I do not do, but what I hate I do" (Romans 7:15).

Our response should be to ask God for forgiveness for our sins and pray for his assurance and assistance in this battle. We are going to sin, but the crucial issue is how we respond to our sin. We may be tempted to blame God, but James wants us to come before God and ask for help. Like David we should pray, "Wash away all my iniquity and cleanse me from my sin....Create in me a pure heart, O God, and renew a steadfast spirit within me" (Psalm 51:2, 10).

Once again it's our attitude and discernment that makes the difference. When desire is conceived through our active encouragement, it gives birth to sin. James wants us to know that sin, when mature and "full grown" becomes a fixed habit leading ultimately to death. "Death" is referring to spiritual separation from God that comes as a result of sin (Romans 6:23; 7:7-12; 1 John 2:16-17; 3:14).

According to an old Chinese proverb, "Sow a thought and reap a deed; sow a deed and reap a habit; sow a habit and reap a destiny." It all starts with a thought. And a thought toyed with long enough ultimately results in action.

Unfortunately, we do not take seriously the corrosive

power of sin within us. When Jesus spoke of the thought of adultery as the same as the act itself (Matthew 5:27-28), he had in mind something similar to what James teaches here. Actions are the result of character, but actions can also shape character.

In the temptation narratives (Matthew 4:7; Luke 4:12) Jesus dealt with temptation through the power of Scripture. Three times he said, "It is written." When you know the Bible, you can detect the bait and deal with it decisively.

To follow Jesus is to learn an attitude of mind and heart that's sensitive to the will and presence of God. The first step is the simple but profound one of opening the door to God in prayer, of asking God to be at work in our minds and hearts, and to change us into his image. "For the Christian," says Richard J. Foster, "heaven is not the goal, it is the destination. The goal is that 'Christ be formed in you.'"

READ BETWEEN THE LINES

- Is there a difference between a trial and a temptation? If yes, what are the differences?
- Is temptation a sin? Explain.
- Who do we blame for temptations in our lives?
- Why should we not blame God?
- What is God's role in temptation?
- Why can't God be tempted?
- What is the true origin of temptation?
- How is a person tempted?
- What are the steps or stages of temptation and sin?

WELCOME TO MY WORLD

- What temptations do I face daily in my life?
- What are some of my "If only..." statements?
- What excuses do I and my friends make for yielding to sin?

- How do I resist temptation?
- Describe a time in my life when I crossed the line.
- What were the consequences?
- Is there something I need to confess to God?

The Father of Lights

James 1:16-17

16Don't be deceived, my dear brothers and sisters. 17Every good and perfect gift is from above, coming down from the Father of the heavenly lights, who does not change like shifting shadows.

Verse 16 could fit with the preceding section as a final warning, closing the preceding sentences. However, most commentators take it as an introduction more closely linking it to the character of God expressed in verses 17-18. It could also be viewed as a bridge between 1:13-15 and 1:17-18. Regardless, James abruptly interjects an exhortation "don't be deceived." The readers are not to be deceived regarding God's character by thinking either that he is the source of temptation or that truly good things have a source other than him.

As a capstone to his argument that God does not tempt anyone, James offers a brilliant picture of the character of God: He is "the Father of the heavenly lights." Since God does not send temptation, the implied question is, "What is it that God does send?" James answers that God gives good gifts, as we have already seen in his gift of wisdom (1:5). Everything good in this world comes from God, even if we do not see the goodness in it immediately (Paul's thorn in the flesh in 2 Corinthians 12:1-10 is an example of this). "Coming down" in verse 17 is a present participle: It keeps coming down. Even when we don't see his gifts God is still sending them.

There is a rich Old Testament background for this idea (Numbers 10:29; Joshua 21:45; Psalm 85:12). Deuteronomy 26:11 speaks of Israelites and aliens together enjoying "all the good things" the Lord has given them. Moses warned Israel not to forget God's goodness when they began to enjoy the blessing of the Promised Land (Deuteronomy 6:10-15).

If King David had remembered the goodness of the Lord, he would not have taken Bathsheba and committed those terrible sins. At least this is what Nathan the prophet told the king. "Thus saith the Lord God of Israel, I anointed thee king over Israel, and I delivered thee out of the hand of Saul; and I gave thee thy master's house, and thy master's wives into thy bosom, and gave thee the house of Israel and of Judah; and if that had been too little, I would moreover have given unto thee such and such things" (2 Samuel 12:7-8). Note the repetition of the word *give* in this brief statement. God had been good to David, yet David forgot God's goodness and took the bait.... God's gifts are always better than Satan's bargains. Satan never gives any gifts, because you end up *paying for them dearly*.

—Warren W. Wiersbe, *Be Mature, James*, 51.

In creating the phrase "Father of the heavenly lights," James has combined two pairs of important theological ideas. The first pair is that God is the Father of the universe (suns, planets, moons), and that he has power over the heavenly luminaries as their creator (Genesis 1:14-18; Psalm 136:7; Jeremiah 31:35); both concepts recall the creation account. The second pair is the notion of God as Father and of God as light. Psalm 19:1, "The heavens declare the glory of God; the skies proclaim the work of his hands."

James further describes God as one "who does not change like shifting shadows." God is light, and in him there is no shadow. God is the creator of the heavenly luminaries, which *do* shift like shadows. In other words, unlike the planets and the stars, which spin and waver, there is no change in God. As Father, God is ultimately reliable. God does not change (Malachi 3:6; Hebrews 13:8), whether in the specific (God is and will always be the one who gives good things) or the general (God is unchangeable and good). God isn't moody and doesn't have bad days. Rather, God is as solid as a rock. God is good all the time.

Clearly James is offering a contrast with astral images. Some commentators argue that James is actually countering a belief in astrological religion and the occult, which believes that lodged in the stars is the power to decode human destiny.

James' readers were apparently seeking to absolve themselves of personal responsibility by claiming they were caught in the unpredictable hands of fate. Perhaps they were influenced by the belief of the ancients that whim, or fate, directed human lives. Mere chance, for example, determined who was born wealthy and who was born a slave. The preeminent deity during this period was *Tyche* (Latin, *Fortuna*), the goddess Fortune or Chance.

The Romans believed that fortune had granted to them the task of ruling the world. In such an environment it is easy to see how persons wishing to blame someone or something else might claim that their misfortune was the product of unpredictable chance. But such a belief does not necessarily imply an astral religion.

To strengthen his point, James points out that God made the heavenly bodies; as if to say that what some call fate is not really fate, for God made and controls the symbols of fate. James even claims that God purposefully intended the creation of both the heavens and of humankind, in order to heighten the contrast between God and an alternative choice of a general belief in fate that held humankind in its mindless changeable grip.

James' point, then, is that ultimately God controls all of the things to which we wrongfully attribute power, whether we do so from ignorance or to avoid responsibility. God supervises and has ultimate power over political forces, economic forces, Satan, fate, and the stars. Perhaps James is contrasting God as Father of the heavenly lights with the pretenders to his throne, the forces of the political order, which are mere shadows, unstable and unreliable.

James 1:18

18He chose to give us birth through the word of truth, that we might be a kind of firstfruits of all he created.

In place of the idea that the destiny of those who follow their evil desire is death, James offers for consideration an alternate path: God, he tells us, "chose to give us birth." The past tense here probably refers to God's creative power and recalls that God made us for himself.

Usually three options are offered for understanding James' phrase, "He chose to give us birth":

1. James has general creation (physical birth) in view;
2. He has the creation of Israel, God's son, in mind (Hosea 11:1: "When Israel was a child I loved him, and out of Egypt I called my son");
3. He's referring to Christian converts (spiritual birth) who are "reborn."

Given the intentional ambiguity of this phrase, it seems most sensible to assume that James was happy to allow his readers to draw upon the rich variety of all three streams, although it is obvious that in the New Testament the third tends to swallow the second.

The agent God used in giving birth to us is "the word of truth." Here is an obvious similarity to John's Gospel, if not a direct link. "Truth" (*aletheia*) is one of the great themes of John's Gospel, and the "word" (*logos*) dominates its prologue (John 1:1-18). John's Gospel claims that "grace and truth came through Jesus Christ" (1:17). In the Old Testament the "word of God" is nearly personified, acting as a characteristic of God himself. The dominant background here is most likely the continuing action of the spoken word of God at creation, the word that accomplishes the purpose of God (Isaiah 55:11). The word of God is God's plan revealing itself and moving to completion. That God chose to give us birth through the word of truth combines images James has already drawn: that God's word is an active force, and that God desires us to be his active partners in accomplishing his purpose. King David said, "I have hidden your word in my heart that I might not sin against you" (Psalm 119:11). The Spirit of God uses the word of God to bring about the miracle of the new birth (John 3:6; 1 Peter 1:23).

The Deuteronomy 26 text is particularly significant, as it appears in the context of the good gifts and firstfruits. It seems certain that James, like Deuteronomy, links the ideas of "good gifts" and "firstfruits" intentionally. The term "firstfruits" is used in a number of ways in the Old Testament. Sometimes, for example, it means certain offerings of Israel; but it can also refer to Israel itself, emblematic of the elect nation whose purpose it is to be a "light for the Gentiles" (Isaiah 42:6) and through whom "all peoples on earth will be blessed" (Genesis 12:3). Here James calls "firstfruits" all who are loyal to God, all who develop into what God calls us to be. Paul can speak of Christian converts as "firstfruits" (Romans 16:5; 1 Corinthians 16:15), and of the risen Christ as the firstfruits of many brothers and sisters (1 Corinthians 12:20).

READ BETWEEN THE LINES

- How are people deceived?
- What are "good and perfect gifts"?
- What are the heavenly lights?
- How is God not like "shifting shadows"?
- How does God give us "birth through the word of truth"? Is this referring to natural birth (Genesis 1:26-27; 2:4-7) or spiritual rebirth (1 Peter 1:23-25)?
- What does it mean to be "firstfruits"?

WELCOME TO MY WORLD

- Describe a "perfect gift" I have received.
- Describe someone I've known or have heard of who's like a shifting shadow.
- When have I been a shifting shadow?
- How does it make me feel to realize God is not like that?
- How thankful am I that God gave me physical and spiritual birth?

Speak Without Anger, Receive the Word in Humility

James 1:19

¹⁹My dear brothers and sisters, take note of this: Everyone should be quick to listen, slow to speak and slow to become angry,

From the word of God (1:18) James turns his attention to human words, and in so doing prepares us for chapter 3, where he will argue that the gift of God's wisdom influences how Christians speak. Believers should concentrate on listening with humility and meekness, rather than speaking in anger.

Immediately we are faced with something of a dilemma. The opening verb, "take note of this" (*iste*), either goes with verse 18—serving as a concluding exhortation to that passage—or as we are likely inclined to agree with other commentators who see it introducing the thoughts to follow. These thoughts are expressed in terms of a proverb.

The idea in verse 19b is nearly universal. Certainly the ancient Greeks knew of it. Dio Chrysostom said, "I for my part should prefer to praise you for being slow to speak, and even more that you are self-controlled enough to keep silent." The passage brings to mind Proverbs 29:20: "Do you see someone who speaks in haste? There is more hope for a fool than for him." (also Proverbs 13:3; 15:1; Ecclesiastes 7:9). James may also have in mind a saying of Jesus: "But I tell you that everyone will have to give account on the day of judgment for every empty word they have spoken" (Matthew 12:36).

Of course as we have seen in James previously, to find parallels to the original meaning of a term isn't the same as discerning the meaning of a text. Some insist that James here is asking his audience to listen to their teachers. While this interpretation has an appeal to preachers and teachers, we can't be certain that a meaning this narrowly focused is true to the historical picture.

In the first century most communication was oral (only 10 to 15 percent of the population could read the little bits of written Scripture that existed), so listening was imperative. Today most of us tend to be poor listeners because of the number of words spoken each day (our minds become numb from overload). Some of us are busy bulldozing and arguing our way through conversations when we should be listening. We also have busy lives and very short attention spans (a scene in a typical television program rarely lasts more than 34 seconds and in cartoons they come every 11 seconds with cuts or fades within a scene coming about every 3 seconds).

We tend to speak much and listen little. There is a time to speak. But there is also a time to be quiet. That's what my father did. Dropping a fly ball may not be a big deal to most people, but if you are thirteen years old, and have aspirations of the big leagues, it is a big deal. Not only was it my second error of the game, it allowed the winning run to score. I didn't even go back to the dugout. I turned around in the middle of left field and climbed over the fence. I was halfway home when my dad found me. He didn't say a word. Just pulled over to the side of the road, leaned across the seat, and opened the passenger door. We didn't speak. We didn't need to. We both knew the world had come to an end. When we got home, I went straight to my room, and he went straight to the kitchen. Presently he appeared in front of me with cookies and milk...Dad never said a word. But he did show up.

—Max Lucado, *Life Lessons, James*, 46.

What's certain is that the passage finds its home in the Jewish wisdom tradition, which placed a premium on measured speech and thoughtful listening. Yet the powerful appeal to community unity in chapter 3 makes it possible that part of the thought here is a plea to peaceful coexistence—being slow to say rash and angry words to others within the Christian community. Zip the lips and suppress the desire to strike back (extinguish the short fuse). Being ticked off and hot under the collar will achieve little. Many church fights are the result of short tempers and hasty words.

It's perhaps helpful to know the problems confronting James' readers. While many of the specifics are lost to us, in 2:1-13; 3:1-4:12 James makes clear a number of the significant ones. The church in the first century was divided over many issues. Some sought to use the church as a means to display wealth and exercise power. Others taught a doctrine of fellowship that denied the centrality of the command to love one's neighbor. Still others had shown obvious favoritism to the wealthy.

Many of us are often guilty of uncontrolled speech, whether an outburst of anger or premeditated gossip. When James says we should be slow to speak, he places his finger on a problem that can have devastating effects. Just as James argues that we should protect the dignity of the poor through material generosity, he also insists that we need to protect everyone's dignity through the way we speak to them. The idea here includes impassioned, spontaneous speech as well as calculated, unrestrained speech, such as gossip. While as children we may have chanted "Sticks and stones may break my bones, but words will never hurt me," the limerick, as recent studies have shown, is untrue. We can get over physical wounds, but many have never fully recovered from hurtful words. Words actually have great power to wound *and* to heal—and we should strive to heal.

> Recently a student sought me out in my office. Over the course of an hour she cried tears of intense pain as she related to me a story. Along with her mother she had visited her aunt, who spoke of her own daughter in glowing terms. The aunt said she wished she could have another daughter just like her.
>
> The mother of my student then voiced a different desire: "I wish that my daughter had never been born."
>
> **—David**

Such speech destroys not only the target, but eventually also the speaker. Gossip can also have tragic consequences. We all know the sting of being made the subject of gossip, and we all have participated in the spread of gossip. Our speech has the power to encourage and nourish life or snuff it out. Which shall we choose?

James 1:20

20because human anger does not produce the righteousness that God desires.

James then turns his attention to two examples that illustrate his point: human anger and the righteous life that God desires. The NIV has, perhaps, placed too soft a garment on the phrase (human anger). James uses the word *ergazetai*, and so the phrase should be translated "for *the practice* of human anger." James seems to have no particular type of anger in view, but puts before us the proposition that anger is damaging to the righteousness God desires of us.

For those who blow their tops and lose their tempers, check out this brief article that appeared in the *Los Angeles Times* years ago: "On the East Side the other night...a man about 55 and his wife quarreled with another driver... over a parking space...bystanders convinced the police that the other driver didn't strike a blow...that the 55 year old punched the other driver twice...he allegedly slugged his wife twice when she urged him to calm down...then he walked ten steps and dropped dead."

It is possible that James is instructing us to be slow to assume the mantle of righteous indignation, because in so doing we implicitly claim to speak for God. Such anger certainly has a rightful place—but should be summoned only after careful and diligent exercise of prayer and thought. James' words concerning slowness to speak are well taken.

James' observation that anger is undesirable can also be found in Proverbs 15:1, "A gentle answer turns away wrath, but a harsh word stirs up anger." More to the point, human anger, which is the product of an underdeveloped willingness to listen, is at odds with God's righteousness.

The chief question here concerns the two possible meanings of "the righteousness that God desires." It can mean:

1. "God's righteous standard"—because God expects us to be above anger, he demands this righteousness of us.
2. "Eschatological righteousness"—that God is the one who will settle all accounts in the end.

This second option enjoys the benefit of a powerful advocate in 5:7-9, for we are told there not to grumble against each other, but instead to wait for the righteous judgment of God when the Lord comes. This has a parallel in Paul: "Do not take revenge, my dear friends, but leave room for God's wrath, for it is written: 'It is mine to avenge; I will repay,' says the Lord" (Romans 12:19).

But the first option is an equally effective candidate, championed by 3:8-12, where Christians are warned against cursing their fellow believers. Both of these are probably in James' mind, and in both cases the same may be said: Outbursts of anger do not produce the kind of righteous behavior God desires to see in our lives. So, we might better paraphrase the sentence, "Righteous action does not spring from anger." We may want to remember the bumper sticker, "Temper is such a valuable thing—it is a shame to lose it."

James 1:21

[21]Therefore, get rid of all moral filth and the evil that is so prevalent and humbly accept the word planted in you, which can save you.

But there is more to it. In verse 21 James speaks in more expansive terms of this life of righteousness. By opening with "therefore" (*dio*, which can also be rendered "according to this principle"), James makes it clear that he is concluding this line of thought. This conclusion opens with a brief series of behaviors that shouldn't characterize the life of a Christian.

Christians should "get rid of" (or "strip off") certain behaviors. Originally this word was used to refer to clothing, and the image of preparation for baptism springs to mind. Further the idea of dying to the old self (Romans 6:3-4) was symbolized by the removal of dirty clothes—"stripping off" the old life. Perhaps James wishes to remind us of the powerful passage in Zechariah 3:3-5, where Joshua the high priest—a symbol for God's people—has his dirty robes removed and is given clean robes, a symbol of God's forgiveness. The verb "get rid of" (*apotithemi*) introduces similar lists of vices in Ephesians 4:25 and 1 Peter 2:1. The word carries with it the idea of total conversion, a complete change of lifestyle.

James instructs us to remove "moral filth" (*rhyparia*) and "evil" (*kakia*). Since this noun "prevalent" (*perisseia*) can also mean "excess" or "surplus," some see James warning only against an "excess" of moral filth and evil. But clearly James wants *no* moral filth or evil present within the Christian community. These terms are among the strongest he has at his command and imply not only general moral evil, but also a premeditated evil intent. Sophie Laws skillfully and helpfully translates the phrase as "all vulgarity and the great mass of malice." The meaning is clear: Christians must turn not only from anger but also from evil and malice, whether random or premeditated.

But turning from evil is not enough. James also places before us an alternative path: "Humbly accept the word planted in you, which can save you." This attitude of humility characterizes the one who has "converted." It's no longer a life of evil and wickedness, but one marked by calm and concern for others. Our attitude is to be one of humility, recognizing God's wisdom relative to our own poor resources in this regard. The way to salvation is to be found in meekness, listening to God's word. Humility is significant not only because it's required for the word to flourish, but also because it's the essential attribute of the poor—those without resources who are dear to the heart of God.

What we are to accept or receive with humility is the word "planted in you." This "word" must be equivalent to the "word of truth" of 1:18, although here it's the true word spoken or read—for 1:22 enjoins us to "listen to the word." The term the NIV renders as "planted" can mean either something intrinsically possessed or something added (engrafted). Which is the best nuance? It's often pointed out that it's logically impossible to accept what one already has; but we should remember that James is concerned primarily with the practical matters. Still he most likely intends both nuances. It's also true that we often fail to take advantage of what we possess. God has granted us new life. It's up to us to learn to live into its awesome possibilities.

James may be borrowing from the Lord's parable of the sower (Matthew 13:1-9, 18-23). Here Jesus compares God's word to seed and the human heart to soil (four kinds: hard, shallow, crowded, fruitful). As members of the fallen human race we need this word of God planted in us and then we must nurture it so that its roots grow deep and strong. But as members of a race originally intended to be in close communion with God, this word has a rightful place within us. It's not an alien agent; rather its implantation is like the rightful return of something needful but long lost. It's necessarily an essential element of those who would be "mature and complete" (James 1:4).

"Save you" can also be translated as "save your souls." "Soul" refers not to the Greek idea of the "higher" or more otherworldly elements of the human person, but rather our whole beings. God's word has the power to save us. We must remember that the New Testament presents a triple pattern of salvation: We *have been saved* through the death and resurrection of Jesus Christ (Romans 8:24-25); we *are being saved* (1 Corinthians 1:18); and we *will be saved* (Romans 8:21-23). This triple pattern helps us understand the shades of meaning that attend to "planted," as it presents us with an image of growth and development. The word of truth has saved us. We are to nurture it, for it is an intentional force in the process of saving us.

While James is often castigated for concentrating on works, we should note how at this critical juncture he carefully highlights the saving power of God's word—and when it grows strong within us, it creates Christian character that results in righteous action.

Certainly contemporary culture exposes us to moral filth, and this requires careful introspection. There's no shortage of candidates for a list of American vices that qualify as "moral filth." Alcohol, drugs, laziness, pornography, abuse, hedonism, premarital sex, adultery, lying, and cheating are but a portion of the candidates.

We often see structural evil as outside of ourselves—a state of being in which we're uninvolved, something perpetrated upon our world by institutions, corporations, or governments. Structural evil is this and more. It includes assumed attitudes and patterns that allow institutions, corporations, and governments to act as if certain evil actions are not evil, or that doing evil is worth the risk, because whatever punishment might be in store is far less severe than the gain to be had. When corporations are fined only $100,000 for excessive pollution of the environment, our values are revealed. How effective a deterrent is a $1,000 fine imposed on a professional basketball player who earns in excess of $5 million annually?

James implores us to hold up to the mirror of God's word not only our personal lives, but also the attitudes, tendencies, and assumptions of our culture. Failure to do so, or to do so only halfheartedly, places us at great risk. Slavery in the American South was defended on biblical grounds, but not legitimately. Is it not reasonable to assume that there are parallel features in contemporary American life?

So, personal evil is linked to structural evil. It's easy to proclaim that abortion is a sin, but until we as Christians understand our responsibility to the unmarried mother living in poverty, we cannot claim the righteousness of God. While many Christians claim that the poor alone are responsible for their condition, we must face the fact that this is a decidedly *American* opinion, based on a decidedly *American* value; it does not reflect the values of the Bible.

James 1:15 exposes us to the idea that sin can grow and flourish. Indeed, one of the curious paradoxical truths about sin is that while it pollutes and destroys, it also propagates itself. One lie often leads to another; children of abusive alcoholics often marry people who become abusive alcoholics.

READ BETWEEN THE LINES

- Who are we to listen to?
- What does God desire from us?

- What is righteousness?
- What things make God angry (Exodus 4:1-17; 32:7-14; Deuteronomy 1:26-36; Zechariah 1:2-4; Mark 3:1-6)?
- Is it ever right to be angry (Ephesians 4:26)?
- What does it mean to "humbly" accept the word?
- How does the word save us?

WELCOME TO MY WORLD

- How am I at listening? (Do I truly listen or do I think about what I'll say next?)
- Why is it so difficult to be a good listener?
- With all of the noises (sounds and words) coming into our ears every day, what filters do we use to sort through it all?
- How can I have ears to hear God this week?
- How can being quick to listen and slow to speak help me be slow to become angry?
- What are my top-three pet peeves that get me angry?
- How do I handle my anger? Do I explode or bury it? Are there other alternatives?
- How can I apply Matthew 5:38-48; 6:14-15 to someone I am angry with?
- What garbage in my life do I need to get rid of?
- How can I stop myself from being polluted by the world's influence?
- What weeds are choking out God's word that was planted in me?

Hearing without Doing Is Worthless

James 1:22

22Do not merely listen to the word, and so deceive yourselves. Do what it says.

Listening is good (1:19). We live in a visually oriented, post-literate society that's unwilling at times to listen. But when we do listen, do we respond to what's been said?

Doing is also good. In Exodus 24:3 we read, "When Moses went and told the people all the LORD's words and laws, they responded with one voice, 'Everything the LORD has said we will do.'" Jesus himself contributed to this tradition: "Everyone who hears these words of mine and puts them into practice is like a wise man who built his house on the rock" (Matthew 7:24).

Judaism and Jesus both understood holiness to be tied to "doing the word," but their radically different definitions of "holiness" led them in divergent directions. For Jesus, the center of God's character is compassion and mercy, as expressed in the twin pronouncement, "'Love the Lord your God with all your heart and with all your soul and with all your strength and with all your mind,' and, 'Love your neighbor as yourself'" (Luke 10:27). However, for his contemporaries, "holiness" had to do with purity and therefore separation from "the world."

Both views of holiness require a life of action, however. James makes this point with the present imperative "do"—continuing to grow in carrying out the commands we hear in God's Word.

Indeed, hearing alone is insufficient. James offers two examples to illustrate his point.

James 1:23-25

²³Anyone who listens to the word but does not do what it says is like someone who looks at his face in a mirror ²⁴and, after looking at himself, goes away and immediately forgets what he looks like. ²⁵But whoever looks intently into the perfect law that gives freedom, and continues in it—not forgetting what they have heard, but doing it—they will be blessed in what they do.

The first is in verses 23-24 in which James turns his attention to a negative example in the form of a proverb: *One who hears without acting is like a man who looks in a mirror and then forgets what he looks like.* Not many people possessed mirrors in the ancient world. The "mirror" in the first century was an item composed of polished metal, usually bronze but sometimes silver or gold. And the "mirror" in James refers to God's word.

James' point is that the image in the mirror—whether the product of a cautious glance or an adoring gaze—quickly dissipates; whatever impression forms in the mind and heart while looking in a mirror is temporary. Imagine seeing hairs on your head out of place, or hairs protruding out of your nose or ears, or a blemish on your cheek, or dirt on your chin and ignoring them.

The second is in verse 25 where James offers a positive example—but this verse is perhaps the thorniest theological problem in the entire letter. One who looks into "the perfect law that gives freedom" and then doesn't forget, but acts upon this vision, is blessed. The phrase "perfect law that gives freedom" may sound odd at first, like a contradiction. Or it may remind us of Psalm 19:7: "The law of the LORD is perfect, refreshing the soul." Elsewhere James calls it the "royal law" (2:8). It's the foundational principle that Jesus spells out in Matthew 22:37-40: "'Love the Lord your God with all your heart and with all your soul and with all your mind.' This is the first and greatest commandment. And the second is like it: 'Love your neighbor as yourself.' All the Law and the Prophets hang on these two commandments."

Isn't a law something which restricts your freedom, which stops you doing what you want?

Yes and no. Supposing we didn't have a law about which side of the road we were supposed to drive on. Everyone would set off and do their own thing. It would be chaos: accidents, near-misses, and nobody able to go at any speed for fear of disaster. The law that says you drive on the left (in Britain and elsewhere) or the right (in America and elsewhere) sets you free. That's what God's law is like: by restricting your "freedom" in some ways, it opens up far greater, genuine freedoms in all other ways.

—N. T. Wright, *The Early Christian Letters for Everyone*, 12.

We think of *law* as something that keeps us from doing what we want or makes us do what we don't want to do. The Bible, however, views *law* more like a sign that says, "Go this way" or "Wrong Way. Do Not Enter"—wisdom that, when followed, results in a life well lived. Not an impediment.

In regard to the person in verse 25 who "looks intently," the verb James uses means to bend over and to peer attentively, examining what it reveals with great care. This word is used twice (John 20:5 and 11), first to describe Peter as he bent over and looked into Jesus' empty tomb, and then Mary Magdalene when she wept and bent over to look inside Jesus' tomb. They both looked with careful, focused consideration.

A mirror allows us to see what we really look like on the outside. Especially those mirrors with that magnifying mirror on one side. Where we see all the imperfections! For most of us our morning face is one we'd just as soon not see.

God's Word is similar to a mirror that gives us an accurate reflection of ourselves. God's Word shows us who we are, warts and all. It tells it like it is. We must examine our own hearts and lives in the light of God's Word. The good news is that in spite of our morning faces, God loves us.

It's not unlikely that James is reflecting the words of Jesus relative to the law. Jesus did not overturn the law of Moses; rather Jesus pierced to the heart of its intention, and in so doing elevated the law. Like Jesus, James doesn't have in mind a new law, but rather the fuller expression of the Jewish law.

Stephen Carter says that law has only two functions:

1. It makes you do what you do not want to do,
2. and it prevents you from doing what you want to do.

This is essentially the problem with Mosaic Law in the eyes of Jesus, James, and Paul. It's somewhat inflexible and, most significantly, *external*. It has little or no power to animate the heart.

In piercing to the heart of the law, however, Jesus touched on the intentions and attitudes that undergird the law. This directed Jesus at times to adopt a more severe stance than the Mosaic Law concerning for example divorce (learn to love and forgive one another; Matthew 5:27-32), and at times a more permissive stance concerning for example Sabbath law (Luke 6:1-11; John 5:1-30).

The person who forgets what he has heard misses the blessing. This blessing may be a promise for the future, as James has already presented the idea of reward (1:12)—or it may be a present blessing. James could have had both definitions in mind.

For James "perfect law" and "word" are related; they are not in opposition, but rather are complementary, for each describes a pattern of how to live out our lives. Many of us were taught that the Jews of the first century kept the law in order to earn the favor of God, but with the death and resurrection of Jesus, we are free from the law. This picture of first-century Judaism has been challenged by many, including E.P. Sanders, who demonstrated in *Paul and Palestinian Judaism* that first-century Jews kept the law not to earn salvation, but as a way of expressing the faith of their salvation.

Simply being Jewish meant that they were already within the sphere of God's grace.

This view is correct, and it's also seen in John the Baptist (Matthew 3:9) and Jesus (John 8:31-41). In both cases the claim of ethnicity (i.e., being related to Abraham) is rendered insufficient. Instead, both John and Jesus say, actions that arise from the heart demonstrate the identity of the true children of Abraham.

The picture of grace versus the law often represents a too-superficial reading of Scripture. Paul says many good things about the law, as even a cursory reading of Romans 2-10 demonstrates. Nor is Jesus free of controversy in this matter. In Matthew 5:18-19, for example, Jesus speaks as a legalist, claiming that not the smallest letter, not the least stroke of a pen, not the least of the commandments will pass away. Similarly in Luke, we encounter a rapid series of teachings about the law. In Luke 16:16 we learn that the law has passed away; in verse 17 we learn that the law can never pass away; and verse 18 enjoins us to an obedience of the law that goes beyond that of the Pharisees.

The cornerstone of Jesus' teaching on the law is that it's a guide, not an impediment. The law is good in that it's a channel that directs us toward living out God's intentions. It's *a* means, not *the* purpose. On its own the law has little if any power to change hearts. For Jesus, strict observance to the letter of the law is not radical obedience. Jesus taught a higher standard of ethical obedience that can't be enforced by any law. He taught an ethic that flows from hearts in tune with God's heart. James points to the same idea with his phrase "the perfect law that gives freedom." We might almost call this a "law of the heart," a growing and innate sense of God's purpose and pleasure in a given situation.

> You may explain 2 Corinthians 3:18 in this way: "When the child of God looks into the Word of God (the glass, the mirror), he sees the Son of God, and he is transformed by the Spirit of God to share in the glory of God!" the word *changed* in the Greek gives us our English word *metamorphosis*—a change on the outside that comes from the inside. When an ugly worm turns into a beautiful butterfly, this is metamorphosis. When a believer spends time looking into the Word and seeing Christ, he is transformed: The glory on the inside is revealed on the outside.
>
> It is this word that is translated "transfigured" in Matthew 17:2. The glory of Christ on the mount was not reflected; it was radiated from within. You will find the same word in Romans 12:2 "Be ye transformed by the renewing of your mind." As we meditate on the Word, the Spirit renews the mind and reveals the glory of God.
>
> —Warren W. Wiersbe, *Be Mature, James*, 65.

The Pharisees attacked Jesus for fraternizing with common "polluted" people. In response Jesus told the crowds to beware the yeast of the Pharisees (Mark 8:15), for they were concerned with outward pollution but ignored its source— hearts out of step with God's heart.

Jesus' dispute, then, was not so much with the law as such but with what he considered a skewed understanding of the law—a tendency to view the law as an end and not the means of some greater good. James agrees. By emphasizing the implantation of the word *prior* to his discussion of behavior, he (like Jesus) presents this "perfect law" or "law of the heart" in descriptive terms. Jesus and James are presenting a picture of life in the kingdom of God.

Neither Jesus nor James are shy, however, about pointing out that the *commands* of God must be followed. These commands are components of the foundation and principles of God's revelation: love for neighbor, forgiveness, preservation of life, and abstinence from idolatry and sexual immorality.

We desperately need to remember the image we see when we peer into the mirror of God's Word. James instructs us to gaze at this mirror and then to remember the image.

> James pleads with us to spend time in introspection, in a careful and accurate gaze in the mirror of the Word, before we sally forth into the world to offer our ill-considered opinions in the name of Christ. Failure to do so can, at times, result in behavior that is unchristian and has the potential to harm others.
>
> If the Lord shows you in the Word that you need to praise Him, don't say, "Good point"—but start praising Him right then! If the Lord shows you in the Word that you need to get right with a brother, don't say, "Someday"—do it right then. Be a *doer* of the Word.
>
> —*Jon Courson's Application Commentary: New Testament Vol. 3*, 1519.

We can study God's Word, meditate on God's Word, discuss God's Word, and memorize God's Word. But the question is: *What has been our response after we have encountered God's message? How have we applied what we have heard?* Check out the examples in the early church of doing what the Bible says (Acts 1:14; 2:42, 46; 13:43; 14:22; 26:22).

READ BETWEEN THE LINES

- What "word" is James referring to?
- What's the point about looking intently in a mirror?
- What is the "perfect law"?
- What often gets substituted for doing the word of God?
- Laws are typically seen as restricting freedom. How can this "perfect law" give freedom?
- What does it mean to "be blessed"?

WELCOME TO MY WORLD

- How has my life changed since I became a Christian?
- How is God's Word a mirror in my life?
- Why is it so easy for me to listen to God's Word without putting it into action?

Pure Religion

James 1:26-27

26Those who consider themselves religious and yet do not keep a tight rein on their tongues deceive themselves, and their religion is worthless. 27Religion that God our Father accepts as pure and faultless is this: to look after orphans and widows in their distress and to keep oneself from being polluted by the world.

Two ties link this section to what's gone before:

1. Verse 26 highlights the sin of rash speech, the theme that opens the passage (v. 19).
2. Here is provided an extension of the idea of "not only hearing but doing good," in that worship is described as worthless without action that's been prompted by godly character.

In both this and the previous section, self-deception plays a significant role. The practice of "pure religion" is described here as the control of speech, acts of charity, and resisting temptation.

One who considers herself religious but cannot keep a tight rein on her tongue is deceiving herself. The word "religious" (threskos) appears in the New Testament only in this spot, though its root word, religion (threskia), is found elsewhere in the New Testament (Acts 26:5; Colossians 2:18). It can refer to inner and outer qualities of worship; generally, however (as here), it points to external ceremonies.

It's unclear what specific practices James has in mind, but like the prophets of old he claims that any religious practice that cannot influence the heart—and therefore, actions—is worthless (Amos 5). James compares the tongue to an animal that must be guided by an iron bit in its mouth (3:4), as we interpret *chalinagogeo* ("keep a tight rein on") found only here in the New Testament. The idea, however, can be found in the Old Testament: "Keep your tongue from evil and your lips from telling lies" (Psalm 34:13). A more specific metaphor is found in Psalm 39:1, "I said, 'I will watch my ways and keep my tongue from sin; I will put a muzzle on my mouth while in the presence of the wicked.'"

James is comparing the tongue to a powerful rearing horse which will take off on a wild ride if the reins are not kept taut. The actions of the tongue will inevitably reveal what's inside its owner. Jesus explained this in a heated exchange with some religious leaders in Matthew 12:34, "You brood of vipers, how can you who are evil say anything good? For the mouth speaks what the heart is full of." James implies not only that rash speech can put one's faith in question, but a "religion" that results in such behavior has insufficient ability to shape the heart—and is therefore worthless.

James then defines pure "religion" that God our Father accepts as looking after orphans and widows and to keep oneself unpolluted by the world. James continues his tribute to the themes of justice and compassion as emblematic of pure religion by choosing a common idea found in the Prophets: *God has special concern for the widows and orphans, as these are representative of all groups in need and open to exploitation.* People at the margins of the social, economic, and legal landscape are always open to exploitation and thereby suffer "distress." James may also have in mind specific conditions of distress that the poor in the Christian community are facing, and he is offering them encouragement and exhortation.

God claims to be the protector of such people: "He defends the cause of the fatherless and the widow, and loves the foreigners residing among you, giving them food and clothing" (Deuteronomy 10:18). Furthermore, in the Old Testament God enlists our participation with him: "Stop doing wrong. Learn to do right; seek justice. Defend the oppressed. Take up the cause of the fatherless, plead the case of the widow" (Isaiah 1:16b-17). We are to care for people who can't care for themselves. In short, *we are to be like God.* It's not without significance, therefore, that James designates God as "Father" here.

The second example of "pure religion" is to "keep oneself from being polluted by the world." In the New Testament the term "world" (*kosmos*) carries broad interpretations. It can mean the created universe, humankind, humankind in need of God's salvation, human-ordered society, or the world order as corrupted and evil, in rebellion against God. Here James uses the word in this last sense—the world as a place of evil and danger.

Wiersbe describes it as a "society without God." But we should not miss the important point that James doesn't teach a removal from the world; rather, he stresses living in the world, but doing so with intelligence and forethought in order to keep one's life, one's reputation, and one's faith pure and secure. For James, true faith enters the surrounding culture but remains free from its evil. Jesus was "without blemish or defect" (1 Peter 1:19), and yet he was the friend of publicans and sinners.

In Judaism the holiness of God was guarded from pollution. In the mind and life of Jesus, however, the holiness of God was robust and strong enough to stride into the mire and muck of human existence. It had a purifying force, able to cleanse the world. James' point is that likewise we are to be purifying agents in the world—but mindful to prevent ourselves from being sullied. In this he is a faithful follower of Jesus.

[Lot] pitched his tent toward Sodom, and then he moved into Sodom. Before long, Sodom moved into him and he lost his testimony even with his own family. When judgment fell on Sodom, Lot lost everything. It was Abraham, the separated believer, the friend of God, who had a greater ministry to the people than did Lot.

—Warren W. Wiersbe, *Be Mature, James*, 67.

READ BETWEEN THE LINES

- How do people who think they are religious contrast with those who are truly religious?
- What does it mean to keep a "tight rein" on their tongues"?
- How can a person keep from being "polluted by the world"?
- What characterizes pure religion?

WELCOME TO MY WORLD

- Who are the needy in my community?
- What am I doing to help them?
- When did I get serious about applying God's Word to my life?
- How can I reach out to the needy?
- Do I see my church favoring the rich over the poor? If yes, how?
- How can I be in the world without being polluted by the world?

Favoritism Forbidden

James 2:1

¹My brothers and sisters, believers in our glorious Lord Jesus Christ must not show favoritism.

James begins chapter 2 with his typical warm address, "My brothers and sisters" (verse 1). James is about to battle an attitude that glorified public pecking orders and produced displays of favoritism in the church. By addressing his readers as "my brothers and sisters," James avoids reference to his own high status and instead makes himself one of and among them.

The world of James was different from our own in that there was almost no possibility of social or economic climbing; the social and economic pyramid was incredibly steep, with virtually no "middle class" as we understand that term. Perhaps 8 percent of the population had "wealth," another 2 percent were gaining it, and the remaining 90 percent lived in conditions that we might describe as "poor."

The opening "our glorious Lord" moves beyond "Jesus is Lord" and even beyond a personal relationship with "Jesus is my Lord" to invoke fellowship so we can say together "Jesus is our Lord." "Glorious" describes the divine nature of Christ, expressed even in his humanity. It seems clear that this statement is a rare case of Christology in the book of James; Jesus Christ is identified with the *Shekinah*, the visible manifestation of the divine. James believes that God is revealed in Jesus—that the appearance of Jesus was and is an appearance of God.

The object of his concern is (*prosopolempsia*) "favoritism," or literally "receiving the face." The believers apparently were judging people based on externals including: physical appearance, status, wealth, and power. The term has its origin in the Old Testament showing unjust favoritism granted to the powerful at the expense of others, often on the part of evil judges (Psalm 82:2; Proverbs 18:5; Malachi 2:9). Favoritism goes against God's royal law to "love your neighbor as yourself" (2:8). As Sophie Laws notes, it's an attitude completely uncharacteristic of God. Whether in church or the hearing of a legal case or some unknown context, the recipients of the letter of James had shown favoritism to those displaying the trappings of wealth.

But Jesus Christ, the very manifestation of God's glory, chose to identify with the poor and the outcasts. On the strength of that model and memory James urges his readers to avoid favoritism, just as our Lord did. In this manner James continues his discussion of the proper way to treat the poor he began in 1:27 with the widow and the orphan. This abuse of the poor is the result of conscious clear action. This abuse can be passive, and may be seen in the total lack of regard the wealthy show to them. In the Roman world the poor were faceless nothings in the eyes of the wealthy.

James 2:2

²Suppose a man comes into your meeting wearing a gold ring and fine clothes, and a poor man in filthy old clothes also comes in.

James then gives a practical illustration or example of this favoritism in the guise of a question. There's no clear reason to believe that this is merely a hypothetical situation; James is most likely referring to an actual circumstance in the life of the community.

The question raised in verses 2-4 suggests the image of two "first-time" guests because they do not know where to sit at a church meeting, and they are only described by their appearance. The first guest is obviously wealthy and not restrained in displaying that wealth. As in the parable of the prodigal son, the ring is a symbol of wealth and status (Luke 15:22).

James is not against wealth; he's against the church becoming an arena for the display of wealth to be used to enhance status. Naming church facilities after donors or other such displays would make James nervous, if not angry. James' teaching is fully in line with that of Jesus in Matthew 6:2-4: "So when you give to the needy, do not announce it with trumpets, as the hypocrites do in the synagogues and on the streets, to be honored by others. Truly, I tell you; they have received their reward in full. But when you give to the needy, do not let your left hand know what your right hand is doing, so that your giving may be in secret. Then your Father, who sees what is done in secret, will reward you."

The second guest is adorned in the grungy, soiled garb of the poor. The two men enter the "meeting." Here is another controversy, for instead of the more usual term *ekklesía* (church), James presses into service the term *synagogé* (synagogue), perhaps indicating an early date of writing for James because in the early days of Christianity, especially, Jewish believers still called the meeting place a synagogue and still worshipped on Saturday, the Jewish Sabbath.

It is interesting that in this illustration the poor man is dressed in shabby (*rhyparos*) clothes (also used in Zechariah 3:3-4 to describe filthy clothes worn by Joshua the high priest, symbolic of the sin of the people). What little we know of ancient mercantilism suggests that all but the wealthy wore homemade clothing. There is no reason to doubt that this was the case in Palestine, too. One of the clearest markers of status in the Roman world was attire.

But Jesus did not look at outward appearances; he looked at the heart. Even his enemies admitted, "You aren't swayed by others, because you pay no attention to who they are." He was not impressed with riches and social status. Jesus was the friend of sinners, though he disapproved of their sins. Jesus ignored national and social differences. We need to treat others as Jesus has treated us. We need to look at everyone through the eyes of Jesus.

James 2:3-4

[3]If you show special attention to the man wearing fine clothes and say, "Here's a good seat for you," but say to the poor man, "You stand there" or "Sit on the floor by my feet," [4]have you not discriminated among yourselves and become judges with evil thoughts?

In verse 3 the question continues: The man who bears the symbols of wealth is shown special attention by being ushered to a fine seat. Matthew 23:6 mentions "the most important seats in the synagogues" (one nearest the *Bema*, the pulpit, the place of the sacred scrolls), while the one who appears poor is ordered to stand in the back, or to sit at the feet of an usher. As Ralph Martin points out, the wealthy person must be a Christian, as the proper fashion to treat pagans would hardly have occasioned such division. The point is that it makes no sense to show favoritism to wealthy Christians just because of their wealth. After all, wealth and status grant to such non-Christians the ability to oppress the church, so it makes no sense for Christians to show favoritism based solely on factors which on other occasions are used to exploit Christians.

In making a judgment based on the appearance of wealth, James says, "have you not discriminated among yourselves and become judges with evil thoughts?" The very question implies that the known and accepted norm within the Christian community was characterized by belief in the equality of all people, especially in political, economic, or social life. The church is the one place where class distinctions (color, political persuasion, financial status, fashion, appearance) should have no place. This church evidently forgot that the ground is level at the foot of the cross. Such an ethic stands in stark contrast with the surrounding culture, which this church is mimicking.

The powerful and wealthy in the first century were accustomed to special treatment, just the sort of favoritism that James here decries. It was not without merit that Jesus spoke of the difficulty of a rich man entering the kingdom of heaven (Matthew 19:23).

James 2:5-7

5Listen, my dear brothers and sisters: Has not God chosen those who are poor in the eyes of the world to be rich in faith and to inherit the kingdom he promised those who love him? 6But you have dishonored the poor. Is it not the rich who are exploiting you? Are they not the ones who are dragging you into court? 7Are they not the ones who are blaspheming the noble name of him to whom you belong?

Ever the pastor, James conveys a stern message with the timbre and tones of gentle tenderness. In Luke 6:20 Jesus proclaims, "Blessed are you who are poor, for yours is the kingdom of God." Standing prominently in the background is the deep Hebrew belief that the poor were especially dear to God.

The phrase "to be rich in faith" indicates that these poor, unlike the rich, not only have "true riches" here in this life, but also eschatological riches, in that theirs is the kingdom. James lays out for us the proposition that it is not their poverty alone which issues forth in the poor's inheritance, but rather the faith that poverty creates.

The grammar and vocabulary clearly describe this poor group in the church—like the individual of undivided mind in chapter 1, they will receive the crown of life which God has promised to those who love him. James also links the poor in general, some of whom when visiting the Christian community experience the same shabby treatment they receive in the world at large. For James this is a great tragedy.

In verse 6 James lets his readers know that the community has "insulted" or dishonored the poor. The question is not concerned with the treatment given the wealthy person, nor is there any hint that James believes membership should be reserved for the materially poor exclusively. The issue is the uneven quality of the treatment, especially since it falls along the same status lines in Roman culture at large. James' point is that to curry favor with others simply because of their wealth is to fundamentally misunderstand the gospel and does injury to the faith. How quickly and easily we have forgotten that each human being we encounter deserves our kindest attention, for each one is made in the image of God.

This insult is rendered all the more unbelievable in that by favoring the rich some in the church have favored the very class of people that sought to take advantage of them and the church, for it is the wealthy and powerful who drag Christians to court.

While almost all commentators wish to see the wealthy as those who "drag" them into court as outside the church, there are several reasons for preferring a different view. Martin's comment—that the fashion in which pagans are to be treated would hardly launch such divisions—is well taken. Further, James' frequent use of "my brothers" must also be considered. Finally, the close association of these three charges (oppression, legal persecution, blasphemy) seems to point to the identification of the wealthy as Christians.

However, if we allow "the wealthy" to stand for the rich both inside and outside of the church, then the objections are largely silenced. Believers have healthier options for settling disagreements, including forgiveness, reconciliation, and restitution, all handled among believers (Matthew 5:23-26; 1 Corinthians 6:1-8).

The "noble name" (verse 7) must, of course, refer to Christ. In the LXX (Septuagint, or the "Greek Old Testament") "the name" was an indirect way of referring to God (Deuteronomy 28:10; Isaiah 43:7). But for Christians the name of Jesus was substituted. In Acts 2:38 Peter says, "Repent and be baptized, every one of you, in the name of Jesus Christ for the forgiveness of your sins." If indeed James is a document of early composition, the fact that it so clearly substitutes the name of Jesus for God is a strong argument that Christian teaching assumed a high Christology at an early date. Given the little Christology that James affords, it's striking that both here and in the ascription of "glory" to Jesus Christ in 2:1 we have statements of high Christology. The rich people are abusing the name of Christ by speaking evil of him or by insulting Christians.

James 2:8

8If you really keep the royal law found in Scripture, "Love your neighbor as yourself," you are doing right.

The third piece of James' argument in verse 8 shows that Scripture doesn't condone favoritism. This is the big gun, a reference to the Law. Nothing was more sacred to a Jew. In contrast to the behavior he has just decried, James holds up the "royal law" found in Scripture. Like Jesus (Matthew 22:37-39), James argues that obedience to the love commandment of Leviticus 19:18 meets the spirit of the entire Old Testament legal body of writings.

The use of "love" in the future tense is indicative of James' hope—a command for future action. To abolish this central tenet of Christian faith—a tenet from Jesus himself—by showing a favoritism that discriminates against the poor is to place oneself alongside those who slander the name of God. This is teaching fully in step with the prophetic tradition in the Old Testament. Isaiah 3:14-15 says, "The Lord enters into judgment against the elders and leaders of his people: 'It is you who have ruined my vineyard; the plunder from the poor is in your houses. What do you mean by crushing my people, and grinding the faces of the poor?' declares the Lord, the Lord Almighty."

The beauty of this law is, of course, that it takes seriously both law and mercy, both sin and grace. God does not "excuse" us from our sin but does forgive us (Romans 1:20; 2:1). To excuse is to claim that the offending party is not, in fact, guilty of the offense, or to deny the seriousness of the offense. To forgive grants full weight to both, and still nullifies the guilt.

James 2:9-10

⁹But if you show favoritism, you sin and are convicted by the law as lawbreakers. ¹⁰For whoever keeps the whole law and yet stumbles at just one point is guilty of breaking all of it.

In verse 9 James goes on to argue that the showing of favoritism is itself sin, and this behavior convicts one of breaking the royal law. According to James, showing favoritism is not a minor transgression or an unfortunate oversight; it is sin. That James regards this sin of favoritism so seriously stands in stark contrast with the apparent lack of concern with which James' Christian audience viewed it. Discrimination against anyone, whether on the basis of dress, race, social class, wealth, sex, etc., is a clear violation of the royal law.

In verse 10 James again echoes the teachings of Jesus when he says that to stumble at just one point of the law is to be guilty in all points. One way to illustrate this is by asking: *How many holes does it take to sink an entire ship?*

For Jesus, sins don't have equal weight; some parts of the law were of greater importance and value than other parts, as his teaching on divorce makes clear: "But I tell you that anyone who looks at a woman lustfully has already committed adultery with her in his heart" (Matthew 5:28). The point James makes here is that the command to love your neighbor as yourself is total: Christians cannot pick and choose who are their neighbors, or when they are to follow this law.

> Where we tend to see God's rules like a fabric, James sees glass. If we throw a small or large stone at the fabric, the hole will be similar in shape and size to the rock thrown. If we throw a stone at the glass, however, any sized stone will shatter the glass. This does not mean that breaking any commandment is just as bad as breaking any other (for example, stealing bread instead of murdering a person). It does mean that deliberately breaking any commandment shows our attitude toward God's direction for our life.
>
> —*Life Application Bible Commentary*, 53.

James 2:11-13

11For he who said, "You shall not commit adultery," also said, "You shall not murder." If you do not commit adultery but do commit murder, you have become a lawbreaker. 12Speak and act as those who are going to be judged by the law that gives freedom, 13because judgment without mercy will be shown to anyone who has not been merciful. Mercy triumphs over judgment.

Verse 11 at first appears to say that committing either murder or adultery makes one a lawbreaker. These two offenses were not chosen haphazardly, for both represent core issues relative to ethical behavior, specifically the honor we bestow to other human beings. Murder clearly is a case of dishonoring the victim, but adultery also, because it demonstrates in unmistakable ways that personal gratification is more important than spouse or children or family.

There is also the possibility that James is speaking literally, that both murder and adultery were known in the community of Christians to which he was writing. The point seems that this discrimination—which at least some in the church view lightly, or even positively—James equates with the most horrific sins.

> It's like the space shuttle. The space shuttle is designed to go up into the heavenlies. But if any one part of it is not functioning properly or is flawed in any way, it won't lift off. So, too, you may not have killed anyone or committed adultery: But if you've lied, your shuttle is grounded.
>
> —*Jon Courson's Application Commentary*, 1524.

In verse 12 we are grateful that God has given us freedom from sin's penalty. Peter adds the constraint: "Live as free people, but do not use your freedom as a cover-up for evil; live as God's slaves" (1 Peter 2:16).

James also links profession and action in verse 12. Here's a strong reminder of the true center of the Christian life—the perfect law planted within us growing strong. It's in actions of self-sacrifice and love that our true faith is demonstrated. In a long passage (Matthew 25:31-46) Jesus says the value of faith is demonstrated in acts of mercy (providing for the hungry, the thirsty, the stranger, the ill-clad, the sick, the prisoner).

There is a judgment. Our words will be judged (Matthew 12:34-37), our deeds will be judged (Colossians 3:22-25), our attitudes will be judged (James 2:13). For both Jesus and

James the law that is the fulcrum of judgment is the law of love for our neighbors.

In verse 13 James continues to follow in the Jesus tradition by arguing that for those who don't show mercy, no mercy will be shown. James points to the danger of allowing favoritism to grow within both the individual and the church. If its growth is not stunted and reversed, this attitude will result in a character nosedive; it will come to dominate future decisions, which will, in fact, affect the eschatological judgment. It is this total failure to live out the implications of the faith that James sees as evidence of no faith at all—faith without works is dead.

It's significant that James ends with a message of hope: Mercy triumphs over judgment. The Old Testament affirms that God is merciful (Exodus 34:5-6), and that people should, therefore, also show mercy to one another (Hosea 6:6). It was a hallmark of the teaching of Jesus (Matthew 5:7; Luke 6:36). A merciful attitude is one of the evidences that a person truly is alive in Christ. The mercy of God is such that he forgives even those who have been guilty of such discrimination—and the mercy that an individual shows has the power to grow strong both in the individual and in the ones shown mercy.

In the movie *The Last Emperor*, the young child anointed as the last emperor of China lives a magical life of luxury with a thousand eunuch servants at his command. "What happens when you do wrong?" his brother asks. "When I do wrong, someone else is punished," the boy emperor replies. To demonstrate, he breaks a jar, and one of the servants is beaten. In Christian theology, Jesus reversed that ancient pattern: when the servants erred, the King was punished. Grace is free only because the giver himself has borne the cost.

—Phillip Yancey, *What's So Amazing About Grace?*, 67.

READ BETWEEN THE LINES

- Define "favoritism" and what are the results of showing favoritism?
- How serious is favoritism according to James?
- What constitutes "special" attention?
- Are these first-time guests or members of the church?
- What are the "evil thoughts"?
- Is James against having wealth?
- How are the poor, rich in faith?
- How did Jesus treat the poor (Luke 5:27-31; 14:12-14; 15:1-7)?
- How are the rich exploiting them?
- How are they blaspheming the noble name?
- Why is it called "the royal law?"
- Are all laws of equal value?
- How is breaking one law as troubling as breaking every law?
- What does it mean "the law that gives freedom"?
- What does it mean to be "merciful"?
- How does mercy triumph over judgment?

WELCOME TO MY WORLD

- Have I ever been poor or rich? What did I learn from that time period?
- Do I feel more comfortable with rich people or poor people? Is this favoritism?
- Have wealth and professional accomplishments become more important than the exercise of the spiritual disciplines as the prerequisite for leadership in my church?
- Where might I be guilty of favoritism and partiality?
- How would I react to someone dressed poorly, unwashed, with bad breath and body odor that entered my church?

- Is it easier for the rich or poor to have faith? Why?
- How is my church caring for the poor, the refugees, the disabled, the disenfranchised, and the broken?
- How closely does my congregation reflect the socio-economic and racial neighborhood in which we gather?
- Would a poor person feel welcome at my church or my school?
- Who can I show mercy to this week?

Faith and Deeds

James 2:14-26 is the one passage where, more than any other, James has achieved notoriety. By all appearances James contradicts the Pauline doctrine of justification, and this constitutes an apparent theological problem. It is for this reason that Martin Luther issued his famous condemnation of James (although as we have seen, Luther has much good to say about various verses in the letter of James as well).

This passage can most easily be divided into four sections:

1. In 2:14-17 he's concerned with the case of the poor Christian who receives only words of encouragement from the church. In James' eyes, this is worthless.
2. In 2:18-20 James makes a rational argument that is difficult to follow—that while some claim the existence of a "true faith" apart from works, such a "faith" is not true but dead and useless.
3. The third (2:21-24)...
4. ...and fourth (2:25-26) sections make biblical arguments supporting the position of James—one involving Abraham; the other Rahab.

James 2:14

¹⁴What good is it, my brothers and sisters, if someone claims to have faith but has no deeds? Can such faith save them?

With verse 14 James turns to the contrast between faith and works. The passage opens with two rhetorical questions: What good is faith without deeds? Can such a faith save them? Both questions expect a negative response. James introduces a fictional "someone" (*tis*) who represents the position James opposes. While this "someone" is fictional, it's clear that the position as stated represents an errant position actually held in the church. The issue is not new in this letter, as it was introduced in chapter 1. *Can authentic faith find expression in a confession of right doctrine alone? Can authentic faith be expressed merely as sentiment that never reaches the point of action? Or is authentic faith by necessity a faith that goes beyond these to include practical action?*

The thrust of James' argument is that such a faith has no value; it does not issue forth in eternal life. The use of the phrase "my brothers and sisters" in both 2:1 and 2:14 indicates that the "brothers and sisters" described in 2:1-13 are guilty of holding to a faith which won't result in eternal life.

The issue not only is moral; it also has implications for salvation. Both Paul and James see faith as a confidence in God's saving act along with the effect of that act in the lives of the followers of Jesus Christ. Neither Paul nor James sees faith as the mere assertion of doctrine. The NIV rightly translates *erga* here as deeds and not works, even though the NIV translates it as "works" in Romans 11:6. Much needless headaches and heartache have resulted from a misunderstanding of this term. Paul often employs "works" to mean "works of the law"; for James "works" means "deeds of Christian righteousness," a practice that Paul would both expect and demand.

The second question of verse 14 is "Can such faith save them?" The faith in view here is *work-less* faith, not faith *per se*. James hates even to dignify this position with the term "faith." Here is another clear link to 2:1-13. Those who show partiality to the rich at the expense of the poor are performing deeds not of faith, but of the wisdom and standards of Roman culture. Faith without deeds is essentially self-interested.

Such a position is not unique to James. Luke 3:7-14 indicates that John the Baptist argued that deeds must accompany true faith. After claiming that faith and deeds go together ("a good tree cannot bear bad fruit, and a bad tree cannot bear good fruit"), Jesus in strong terms warned that many who call him "Lord" will not enter the kingdom of heaven (Matthew 7:15-23). The priest and the Levite in the parable of the good Samaritan each had religious training, but neither of them paused to assist the dying man on the side of the road (Luke 10:25-37).

James 2:15-17

[15]Suppose a brother or a sister is without clothes and daily food. [16]If one of you says to them, "Go in peace; keep warm and well fed," but does nothing about their physical needs, what good is it? [17]In the same way, faith by itself, if it is not accompanied by action, is dead.

James in verse 15 then gives an illustration from the life of the church. The people described don't even have simple, basic needs of life (food and clothing). Here James envisions a situation in which church members fail to display even the most elementary forms of charity to one another.

From this example James will build his case. In verse 16 James surprises his readers with a response that seems unbelievable, giving a group of empty greetings or blessings: Go in peace! Keep warm! [Be] well fed! The serious charge that James offers here represents a failure to meet others' basic needs.

James is not alone in these thoughts. The apostle John agrees: "If anyone has material possessions and sees a brother or sister in need but has no pity on them, how can the love of God be in that person?" (1 John 3:17).

In verse 17 James describes faith without works as dead (*nekra*). By this James means, of course, that it is useless, ineffective, and powerless to accomplish the aim of true faith. It is striking that James appears to grant even less value to this "faith" than the "faith" of the demons mentioned in 2:19.

James Ropes notes the contrast is not so much between faith and works but between dead, useless faith and living faith. Faith without works is as dead as a body without breath. Works are not something extra to be added to faith; works are a necessary part of faith—without works faith is not really true faith; it is only a shadow of true faith.

James clearly teaches that faith without works is dead (James 2:17). Give an example of what a person's life might look like in one of these scenarios:

- A person who has faith but no works
- A person who has works but no faith
- A person who has faith in God and works that grows naturally out of this faith
- A person who has no faith and no works

Which of these four scenarios best describes where you are in your life right now?

—Bill Hybels, *New Community, Live Wisely, James*, 42.

James 2:18-20

¹⁸But someone will say, "You have faith; I have deeds." Show me your faith without deeds, and I will show you my faith by my deeds. ¹⁹You believe that there is one God. Good! Even the demons believe that—and shudder. ²⁰You foolish person, do you want evidence that faith without deeds is useless?

In this section James offers a rational argument in order to show that while there may be a type of "faith" which does not issue forth in works, such faith is dead; it has no saving power. True faith, James here insists, always changes the heart and therefore results in acts of mercy and compassion.

In verse 18 an unnamed "someone" is quoted. There

are several options as to where to place the parentheses; the one that seems to fit best is offered by Ralph P. Martin that James resumes speaking midway through verse 18 as the NIV indicates, "Show me your faith without deeds..." According to this view James challenges his opponent to demonstrate faith apart from works, which, of course, is impossible. James then would demonstrate faith through works. This is consistent with the thought of the epistle: Only faith that issues forth in deeds is true faith.

In verse 19 James remarks that to believe there is one God is an excellent starting point. This person has the basic theology down. Monotheism (one God) is perhaps the most fundamental of all Jewish beliefs. It is contained in the *Shema*, the customary Jewish confession based on Deuteronomy 6:4: "Hear, O Israel: The LORD our God, the LORD is one."

But such an intellectual conclusion, while good, is not true faith; for even the demons know this much and "shudder" (*phrisso—to bristle up like a frightened cat*), which occurs only here in the New Testament. The demons might be better off than the so-called Christians James is addressing in that the demons at least have some reaction to their confession. As R. Kent Hughes has said, "There isn't a demon in the universe who is an atheist." Both James and his opponents believe that a faith with deeds exists and is a saving faith, but James cannot agree with his opponents that there is also a saving "faith" that exists without deeds.

The scornful nature of James' response is captured in verse 20 with his use of "foolish" (*kene*), as the term can mean both foolishness and deficient moral standing. This foolish person's faith has not penetrated his heart or made its way down to his hands and feet. Religion that is worth something involves action which grows from the heart. This view has the advantage of nicely picturing those members of the Christian community who refuse to offer concrete assistance to the poor. Instead they show favoritism by offering only pious verbal nothings. James even makes his point with a bit of humor in the form of a word play: Faith without works (*ergon*) does not work (*arge = a + ergos*).

James 2:21-24

21Was not our father Abraham considered righteous for what he did when he offered his son Isaac on the altar? 22You see that his faith and his actions were working together, and his faith was made complete by what he did. 23And the scripture was fulfilled that says, "Abraham believed God, and it was credited to him as righteousness," and he was called God's friend. 24You see that a person is considered righteous by what they do and not by faith alone.

Here James employs the example of Abraham to demonstrate the linkage between faith and deeds. It is possible that the opponent(s) of James had cited Genesis 15:6, where it is said that God reckoned righteousness to Abraham because Abraham believed. James, understanding the revered status of Abraham wishes to point out that the faith of Abraham was not a sterile intellectual assent, but rather one that manifested itself in trusting actions which often involved great risks, such as the near-sacrifice of Isaac.

Philo claims that Abraham's offering of Isaac was the greatest of Abraham's "works" (*Abraham*, 167). James may also have in view, though not specifically mentioned, the hospitality which Abraham showed to the three travelers in Genesis 18. Abraham did acts of mercy because of his faith in God; his deeds flowed out of his faith in God.

James here presents a thoroughly Jewish notion of righteousness; that is righteousness is nothing if it is not about conduct (Isaiah 43:9; Matthew 12:37; Romans 2:6-11;

6:1-12). Righteousness that is true will always compel the righteous to acts of mercy and kindness (Romans 2:7).

Those familiar with the letters of Paul can see a problem here. In Romans 3:28 Paul says "For we maintain that a person is justified by faith apart from the works of the law." But in James 2:24 we read, "You see that a person is considered righteous by what they do and not by faith alone." Once we move beyond the superficial the evidence will show that Paul and James are in essential agreement.

Words can carry various meanings; Paul and James intend different meanings in their use of the same terms. For Paul as well as for James "faith" means acceptance of the gospel and includes a personal commitment to Jesus Christ and his mission. James argues that faith results in acts of Christian love which are the fulfillment of the royal law.

Paul believes that the justification granted to Abraham is the result of the promises of God given to Abraham (Romans 4:1-5; Galatians 3:6-7). Justification is something God *did*, absent any worthiness on the part of Abraham. James, by contrast seizes upon the near-sacrifice of Isaac. This is an example of Abraham's faith, a *present* demonstration of what God had *done* in Abraham.

The question is whether or not the Pauline view is consistent with the view of Jesus. It was Jesus who said, "Each tree is recognized by its own fruit" (Luke 6:44). It was Jesus who said that many will say, "'Lord, when did we see you hungry or thirsty or a stranger or needing clothes or sick or in prison and did not help you?' He will reply, 'Truly I tell you, whatever you did not do for one of the least of these, you did not do for me.' Then they will go away to eternal punishment, but the righteous to eternal life" (Matthew 25:44-46). The standard here is the equivalent of James' "deeds."

In the New Testament generally, and in Paul's letters, salvation is a threefold experience (see also our commentary on 1:21):

- It is first an accomplished fact. We have been saved (Ephesians 2:8).
- Second, it is a present experience. We are being saved (1 Corinthians 1:18; Philippians 2:12).
- Third, salvation is a future hope. We will be saved. (Romans 13:1; Philippians 3:20).

Part of the difficulty in rectifying the Paul-James question over deeds is that Paul in Romans 3:28 is speaking of salvation as a past event. Nothing human beings can do will earn God's forgiveness. James, when speaking of deeds, has in mind present activity. Paul's teaching about faith and works focuses on the time before conversion, and James' focus is after conversion.

Between James and Paul there is no disagreement of substance, but only one of vocabulary and emphasis. Paul was trying to argue against a false doctrine that claims works of the law apart from faith lead to salvation. James does not see faith by itself as deficient; rather he argues that true faith always results in deeds. Check out the Hall of Faith in Hebrews 11:4-29 which R. Kent Hughes has pointed out is also the Hall of Works. Jon Courson mentions that, "It is not faith *and* works that saves a person. Neither is it faith *or* works. It is faith that works." Someone once said that faith is like calories: You can't see them, but you can always see the results!

Back to the passage (2:21), the use of "our Father" to refer to Abraham is often taken to mean that both the author and audience are Jewish. However, Clement calls Abraham "our Father" in addressing an audience of predominantly non-Jewish Christians (1 Clement 31:2). In any event, such a statement would be natural if even a significant minority within the church were Jewish Christians.

In verse 22 the faith of Abraham was made complete through his works. The term for "made complete" is *eteleiothe*, derived from the same root as "mature and complete" in James 1:4. James wants to hold that both faith and works must mix together for either to be worthwhile. We can never be "made complete" without both.

In verse 23 the use of the connective "and" is meant to show that Genesis 15:6 is proof of the accuracy of the position James has advocated. By showing that the faith of Abraham was faith because his trust was active, James has undercut the possibility of seeing Genesis 15:6 as supporting an exclusive "faith alone" position. Abraham's "faith-work," James argues, is the type of faith that God considers righteous.

The designation "called God's friend" is not found in the Old Testament, but in Isaiah 41:8 we read God referring to Abraham as "my friend," and the phrase "God's friend" is similar to the phrase "Abraham your friend," by which Jehoshophat referred to Abraham in 2 Chronicles 20:7. The word friend (*philos*) is the same one Jesus used. Jesus stated that an ingredient of friendship is obedience: "You are my friends if you do what I command" (John 15:14). Jesus' commands included "Do not let your hearts be troubled. You believe in God; believe also in me" (John 14:1). Acting out our trust in God will lead to friendship with him, as it did with Abraham.

The statement in verse 24 is the natural conclusion to what he has said concerning Abraham. Here James is as close to contradicting Paul as at any other juncture in the letter. Yet it is important to see that James is actually defending a Pauline position. James does not wish to set "faith" and "deeds" at odds, nor does he wish to deny the importance of faith in justification. His point is that each needs the other in order to be effective. Faith alone is not sufficient, says James. This is the natural equivalent to Paul's formula of "faith expressing itself through love" (Galatians 5:6). A person receives salvation by faith alone, not doing works of obedience; but a saved person does deeds of righteous obedience because of that faith. D.L. Moody often said, "Every Bible should be bound by shoe leather."

James 2:25

25In the same way, was not even Rahab the prostitute considered righteous for what she did when she gave lodging to the spies and sent them off in a different direction?

Here in verse 25 James uses the example of Rahab to buttress his claim concerning the unity of faith and deeds. Rahab is the polar opposite of Abraham: the patriarch and the prostitute (some less significant translations suggest "innkeeper"), the revered founder of the Israelite nation and the pagan, immoral woman. Rahab lived in the city of Jericho at the time when the Israelites, on their way to the Promised Land, were about to cross the Jordan River with Jericho as their first target. Joshua sent two men, ahead of his invasion, to spy out the city. They stayed the night in Rahab's house. She protected them from the troops who were looking for them, explaining that she had come to believe the "LORD your God is God in heaven above and on the earth below" (Joshua 2:11). The point is she translated her belief into action.

In the early Christian book 1 Clement, Abraham and Rahab are placed together as examples of hospitality. Because by faith she welcomed and hid the Jewish spies (Joshua 2) and Abraham received the three strangers who brought him news of God's promise (Genesis 18).

Rahab's actions were evidence of faith. In Jewish tradition Rahab married an Israelite and became the ancestor of Jeremiah and Ezekiel, and in the Christian tradition is included as one of four women mentioned in the genealogy among the ancestors of Jesus (Matthew 1:3-6).

The Bible describes neither Abraham nor Rahab as

perfect. In fact, the spotlight shines on their sins as much as on their trust. Rahab's courageous action was to show hospitality to the spies (Hebrews 11:31), just as Abraham was courageous when he was willing to trust God in obedience when asked to sacrifice his own son (and his hospitality to the three strangers). These examples are perhaps chosen because the church has refused to show hospitality to those whose outward appearance would indicate that they had no ability to be of benefit to the church. Yet both Abraham and Rahab showed hospitality to those whose outward appearance mirrored the poor in the church to whom James writes.

> O it is a living, busy active mighty thing, this faith. It is impossible for it not to be doing good thing incessantly. It does not ask whether good works are to be done, but before the question is asked, it has already done this, and is constantly doing them. Whoever does not do such works, however, is an unbeliever. He gropes and looks around for faith and good works, but know neither what faith is or what good works are. Yet he talks and talks, with many words, about faith and good works.
>
> —Martin Luther's preface to the epistle to the Romans in 1552.

James 2:26

²⁶As the body without the spirit is dead, so faith without deeds is dead.

With verse 26 James offers his conclusion to the entire passage. In Greek thought there can very easily be a division between the body and the spirit. However, in biblical thought this idea has no place. "Flesh" in Hebrew is *basar*, whether living or dead. *Nepesh* (or "soul") is what makes a body living. A Greek might say, "I have a soul," but in strict biblical thought we should say, "I am a soul."

So James here is a good biblical theologian. He argues

that just as *nepesh* describes a living body, so faith is properly used to describe a trust in God that by definition is marked by faithfulness of behavior. The examples of Abraham and Rahab have been provided to make the case indisputable. When the Spirit and wisdom of God are ours, our hearts are changed, and so then, are our desires and our actions.

The contrast James has made is not between faith and works, but between genuine faith and false faith. James issues a call to Christians that is simple, yet awesome in its scope. What good is faith if you turn your back, or close your eyes, to others in need? Where are the Abrahams and the Rahabs?

> Margaret Dix is a classy lady. She and her husband Howard would be considered two of the pillars in the church where I was a youth minister for 22 years. They are also two of the kindest, most servant-hearted people I know. We had an occasional homeless guy who started attending our church. He was overweight, hair disheveled, hadn't shaved in a while, terrible teeth, his breath caused you to take a step or two back as he talked, the clothes he wore were so dirty it was hard to tell the original colors and worst of all you could smell him 50 feet away. After he started attending our church Margaret invited him to their lovely Orange County home for lunch. She washed his clothes (twice) and let him take a shower in their home. She treated him with dignity and respect. May her tribe increase.
>
> —Les

READ BETWEEN THE LINES

- What is faith that is dead?
- Is this the same as having only an intellectual faith? Explain.
- What kind of faith do demons have? Why is this not enough?

- What kind of faith is James writing about?
- How are Abraham and Rahab examples of faith that works?
- How do you explain the differences and similarities between the apostle Paul and James when explaining faith and works?
- "It is easier said than done" is an old cliché. How does it apply to this teaching by James?

WELCOME TO MY WORLD

- Do I talk more about the poor rather than doing things for the poor?
- Abraham held nothing back from God. Am I holding anything back from God?
- How have I cared for those in need?
- Am I feeling overwhelmed with all the images from modern media describing those in need? What is one thing I could do?
- What has God been asking me to do that I have been ignoring?
- How should I respond to others whose faith and actions are far apart?
- How has my faith changed how I treat people?

Taming the Tongue

James 3:1

¹Not many of you should become teachers, my fellow believers, because you know that we who teach will be judged more strictly.

It can be said of James 3:1-12 that no other portion of the Bible speaks with greater clarity and power on the potentially destructive power of our words. This passage makes three basic points:

1. Small items, such as the tongue, a rudder, or even one teacher, can and often do control a larger whole, such as the body, a ship, or the entire congregation.
2. One source of this evil is hell, the stronghold of Satan.
3. When the tongue is influenced by the forces of hell, the result is severe double-mindedness. This irrationality is seen in the same tongue praising God but cursing other people, who have been made in God's likeness.

The connection between this section and those before is not immediately obvious, yet it is there. While it is true that James introduces a new notion by discussing teachers, the heart of this section, like that found in 1:19-21, has to do with proper speech. James launches upon this discussion because a verbal attack, like favoritism, has a particularly corrosive and lethal effect upon the life of a community of faith. The community is no distinct community at all, but merely another avenue to personal power like so many others in the Roman world at large.

Another source that binds this section to what has gone before is the frequent use of the term "the body" (*soma*). It first appears in reference to the tongue as a part of the human body, but quickly James uses it to refer to the Christian community.

Earlier we noted that the opening of the letter is concerned with personal morality, but with chapter 2 James concerns himself with corporate morality, and that continues to be the case.

James 3:1 begins with a negative in order to emphasize the serious danger associated with the office of teacher. Being a rabbi or teacher was the highest calling of a Jewish child. Teachers had great influence and status in the early church (Ephesians 4:11). The responsibilities of teaching in the context of the church are serious, so serious that great deliberation ought to accompany the desire to teach. It is also possible, given what James is about to say, that some who have exercised that function ought to lay it aside. James takes pains to show that he is quite aware of these demands, for he is a teacher, as the second clause (we who teach) demonstrates. It should be noted that the New Testament church had a dire need for teachers, but little recourse when it came to examining the qualifications and testing the orthodoxy of these teachers.

The reason for James' warning here is that teachers receive a more strict judgment if they fail. It is not unlikely that James has in mind the teaching of Jesus recorded in each of the Synoptic Gospels: "If anyone causes one of these little ones—those who believe in me—to stumble, it would be better for them to have a large millstone hung around their neck and to be drowned in the depths of the sea" (Matthew 18:6; Mark 9:42; Luke 17:2). James does not specifically identify the judgment he has in mind, but given the teaching of Jesus just cited, it is logical to assume that James has in mind the eschatological judgment.

By nature of their position teachers have an inordinately greater opportunity to influence others within the congregation. It seems unavoidable that James is blaming certain teachers in the community for teaching false practices, such as favoritism and an erroneously anti-law attitude. Having dealt with each error, he now focuses on the source of those errors, the false teachers themselves. James probably has in mind another of Jesus' teachings: "But I tell you that everyone will have to give account on the day of judgment for every empty word they have spoken" (Matthew 12:36). These words are careless not simply because they are spoken in a thoughtless moment, but because unlike the word of God, they are not able to accomplish their purpose. The doctrine and practice advocated by these teachers do not contribute to the edification of the community, but instead are detrimental.

Teachers wield incredible power in crucial times and over tender lives. In the hands of a skilled teacher students are like clay in a potter's hands. Casual advice from a teacher can direct the course of a student's whole life.

I didn't become a Christian until my junior year in high school. Soon after I started helping out with the younger children in our small church, and I loved it. When I started going to Santa Monica City College, I helped in the junior high and high school group. One day Harry Bucalstein, the senior pastor of the church, noticed my enthusiasm in working with students and made a comment that literally changed my life. He simply said, "I think you would make a great youth minister." I did not have many conversations with Mr. B (as we called him), but I could not get that one out of my head. He began to encourage me to use the gifts he felt God had given me, and by the next semester I was enrolled in a local Christian college studying to be a youth minister. His kind and encouraging words set the course for my life for the next 45 years. Because of him every time I meet a teenager or college student, I try to say something encouraging to them because you never know what will come of it.

—Les

Within the early church the position of teacher was one of high status. We have already seen that the very human desire for status was prevalent in the Roman world. For most of Roman history the way to gain status and power was through making a reputation during battle. With Augustus, however, came the famous Roman peace. Opportunities to gain a reputation were therefore significantly reduced. What happened was a proliferation of private clubs or associations called *collegia*. People joined these for a sense of association and for the chance to have a position of honor. Many thought the Christian church was just another of these clubs, and sought for themselves power and honor in the church. The role of teacher was one such people prized, as it came with authority and honor. Teachers do deserve respect, and the respect granted to teachers within Judaism ought not to be ignored. The Talmud relates that one year on the eve of the Day of Atonement a crowd was escorting the high priest to his home. Having spied two scribes, the crowd left the high priest in favor of the scribes.

The danger occurs when the ambition to teach comes out of a false motive of public attention. This ambition reaches its peak when it begins to envy others. Jesus said in Matthew 23:5-7, "Everything they do is done for people to see: They make their phylacteries wide and the tassels on their garments long; they love the place of honor at banquets and the most important seats in the synagogues; they love to be greeted with respect in the marketplaces and to be called 'Rabbi' by others." As Paul describes in Philippians 1:17, "The former preach Christ out of selfish ambition, not sincerely, supposing that they can stir up trouble." James is discouraging taking up the role of teacher for wrong motives.

Unfortunately, there was evidently a serious problem with taking up the role of teaching for the wrong motives in the early church. Without any clear standards, anyone could be put forward as an authority, and even Paul was challenged on this matter. James, like Paul, issues a plea to accept his authority as paramount over his opponents. But he does so in a fashion not reminiscent of Paul.

James 3:2

2We all stumble in many ways. Anyone who is never at fault in what they say is perfect, able to keep their whole body in check.

In verse 2 James admits a very human truth—none of us is perfect; we all stumble and mess up from time to time. But it will happen less often if we learn to discipline our tongue and take control of our conversations. The word "many" might refer either to the number or the variety of sins, but it most likely refers to both. Yet there's at least one sin that's common to all—the sin of the tongue. At this point James has in mind not only teachers, but all Christians—although, of course, the effects of a stumble in the case of teachers can have far wider effects.

But if, as James imagines, there was someone who never sinned in speech, then that person would be perfect. The notion of a perfect man (*teleos aner*) must be that of completeness and maturity, just as in 1:4. This is completeness in Christian virtue, not sinlessness.

To keep their whole body "in check" implies control of the passions. The expression also means "to bridle," which introduces the analogies James uses next. Speech—and especially the tongue as emblematic of speech—is often the tool of the *yeser ha-ra* (the evil impulse).

James 3:3-4

3When we put bits into the mouths of horses to make them obey us, we can turn the whole animal. 4Or take ships as an example. Although they are so large and are driven by strong winds, they

are steered by a very small rudder wherever the pilot wants to go.

The wisdom tradition has much to say concerning the untamed tongue. Proverbs 16:27-28 says, "A scoundrel plots evil, and on their lips it is like a scorching fire. A perverse person stirs up conflict, and a gossip separates close friends" (see also 10:8, 11, 19; 18:7, 8). But there's more than this at work here, for James has in mind teachings that have the effect of leading people astray, to teach theological untruth as if it were truth. James insists that someone who's faultless in what he says is able to bridle (*chalimago*—the same word that was used in 1:26) his body.

His point made a number of times in this section is that a small item (e.g., the bit, the rudder, the tongue) can guide and control the larger whole. It should not be lost on us that those teachers (and other leaders) in the church fit this image nicely. The same small member can either guide the larger whole to safety or condemn it to the ravages of meanness and falsehood.

In verses 3-4 James begins a series of illustrations from everyday life meant, in part, to bring home to his readers with especially keen vividness the power of the tongue. The first two analogies are not quite precise (the tongue does not control the body in the fashion that a bit controls a horse or a rudder a ship), but the meaning is plain enough.

The tongue is like the bit in a horse's mouth. With small ropes and a small one-pound piece of metal, a bit may seem at first insignificant—but with it a rider can control the movement of a 1,500-pound horse. In the fifth century B.C. playwright Sophocles has one of his characters say, "I know that spirited horses are broken by the use of a small bit."

The tongue is also like the rudder on a ship. Great ships driven by strong winds are steered by a relatively small rudder. Modern mammoth cruise liners (basically huge, floating hotels) are also controlled by a comparatively diminutive piece of metal.

> Early in the Second World War a shell from the German battle-ship *Bismarck* sunk the heavy cruiser *Hood*, the pride of the British navy. A great chase commenced, and the *Bismarck* was finally doomed when a torpedo destroyed its rudder, causing it to sail haplessly in circles until a barrage of British naval artillery sent her to the bottom of the Atlantic.
>
> **—Winston S. Churchill, *The Grand Alliance*, Houghton and Mifflin Co., Boston, 1950, 315-319.**

The church in turn is controlled by those in leadership roles. Thus, just as the rider directs the horse and the pilot the rudder, so the Christian teacher must be under the direction of the proper authority.

James 3:5

[5]Likewise, the tongue is a small part of the body, but it makes great boasts. Consider what a great forest is set on fire by a small spark.

In verse 5 James displays some of his literary skill, particularly alliteration: The tongue is a small (*mikron*) member (*mélos*) but boasts of great things (*megála*). James claims that the tongue makes boasts, and boasting in the New Testament is generally considered a sin, as it indicates a desire to place oneself in the role of God.

When the tongue is out of control it can destroy the good work that has already been done; a leader whose teaching is errant can in short order devastate years of careful and healthy growth in the life of a congregation. Such teaching was threatening the community to which James writes. He had to bring it to a stop and steer the community in the right direction.

Leonardo da Vinci's giftedness as a master sculptor led him to study the human body in as much detail as any physician of his day. When he began describing the tongue (which rarely appears in either his paintings or his statues), he noted, "No member needs so great a number of muscles as the tongue; this exceeds all the rest in the number of its movements." Indeed, the tongue is small but extremely powerful. James wants to impress this very fact on our minds so we won't underestimate the effects it can have—both positively and negatively.

—Charles R. Swindoll, *Swindoll's New Testament Insights on James, 1 & 2 Peter*, 68-69.

Peter Davids points out how James executes a shift in tone: Both the bit and the rudder were discussed in positive terms, but here the tongue is discussed in negatives. This is because the potential of the tongue is so much greater than that of the bit or the rudder; it's capable of sublime heights, but also of sinking to the wicked depths of evil. James' point is that we shouldn't underestimate the powerful potential of leadership positions nor the damage that can be done through careless or mean-spirited speech.

James then turns to a new image: That of a fire set by a small spark. Across America each summer we know all about the destructive power that can come from one carelessly lit match. Legend has it that at 9 p.m. on Sunday, October 8, 1871, poor Mrs. O'Leary's cow kicked over a lantern as she was being milked, starting the Chicago fire, which blackened three and a half miles of the city—destroying more 17,000 buildings, leaving more than 100,000 people homeless—before it was checked by gunpowder explosions on the south line of the fire. The inferno lasted two days and claimed more than 250 lives.

James asserts that the devastation caused by an uncontrolled fire is similar to what the unmonitored tongue can do:

It can soil a person's character, ruin a reputation, and even devastate a church. And the damage can be far reaching. A careless word, a nasty rumor, a bit of slander—can damage a person many miles away from the source. Once the "spark" is dropped and the fire starts, the damage is done.

Although there are clear parallels in Greek literature, the background for this saying is found in Jewish literature. The wisdom tradition especially has much to say about the destructive power of the tongue, at times associating the tongue with images of fire. Proverbs 26:21 says, "As charcoal to embers and as wood to fire, so is a quarrelsome person for kindling strife" (see also Proverbs 16:27; Psalm 39:1-3, 120:2-4). Few disasters in the ancient world were more feared than fire, as the ancients possessed precious few resources to battle them, even in urban centers. The point of the image is to emphasize the great destructive power of the tongue.

In one of his letters to Trajan, Pliny makes mention of an urban fire: "While I was inspecting another area of the province, a fire in Nicomedia consumed many private homes and two public buildings, the club for elders and the temple of Isis, even though a road runs between them. It was encouraged at first by a breeze, but it would not have been so violent were it not for the uncaring attitude of the citizens. It seems people stood and watched the disaster, immobile, doing nothing to stop it. Nor is there even one fire engine in town, nor a bucket, not any other instrument for fighting a fire."

—Pliny, *Epistulae*, X, 33.

James 3:6

[6]The tongue also is a fire, a world of evil among the parts of the body. It corrupts the whole body, sets the whole course of one's life on fire, and is itself set on fire by hell.

In blunt fashion, using some of the strongest terms at his command, James makes clear in verse 6 the effects and source of an errant tongue. At this point it's evident that both levels of meaning are in play: The uncontrolled tongue can cause great harm, and Christian teachers whose teaching in the church is errant have caused great harm.

But beneath the apparently obvious meaning is great complexity. Many of the phrases are puzzling at best. In addition, the text is marked by a number of variant readings, which has led some commentators to conclude that the original text has been corrupted. There is no denying the fact that this passage is difficult to interpret, but we must follow it.

Regarding the "world of evil," James chooses to use *kosmos* (world)—a term rich in various meanings. The linkage of this word with "evil" suggests that of the many nuances assigned to *kosmos* in the New Testament, here it must mean the world and its forces opposed to God. A variety of characters inhabit this world, and it's clear that James believes that the false teachers are citizens of that world—or at least under the influence of that world, even if they lack self-awareness.

The point that James wishes to make is that the great "world of evil" is seen in smaller, specific examples. On one level the uncontrolled tongue is an example of this world—evil and opposed to God; on another level the teachers opposed to James are examples of this same world. Neither the tongue nor the teachers are guided by the Spirit of God, but just as the rudder is controlled by the pilot, the uncontrolled tongue and the false teachers are guided by the forces of hell.

There are other grammatical difficulties with this verse. The NIV understands "a world of evil" as grammatically connected to the opening phrase "the tongue is a fire." Most commentators disagree, claiming that the verb "to be" should be understood in the opening phrase, which then becomes a complete sentence. This has the advantage of allowing both occurrences of *glossa* ("tongue") to register in translation: "And the tongue is a fire. The tongue is a wicked world present among our members." But, as Martin points out, there is really little difference between the two translations. The point is that the tongue often is guilty of realizing its potential for evil and in so doing infects the rest of the body.

This, in fact, is what James says at the end of verse 6, that the tongue can corrupt or stain the entire person (*soma*; literally "body"). Here's another way of making a point James has already registered: Although small, the tongue controls the larger whole (3:2, 3, 4). James continues his series of negative comments about the tongue, stating that it "sets the whole course of one's life on fire." That is, the tongue can corrupt all of life, whether the life of an individual or of a community. Given the double narrative of the entire passage, James most likely intends this ambiguity.

In his phrase "is itself set on fire by hell," James traces the root of the evil, the mouthpiece of which are the teachers, and the expressions of which are (particularly) favoritism and antinomianism (against law). The Greek word translated "hell" is *geenna* (usually transliterated as "Gehenna"), which referred to *Ge Hinnom*, the valley south of Jerusalem that had become a symbol of evil and was thought of as a stronghold of Satan. It seems clear that James is arguing that Satan is the ultimate source of the corrosive false teachings offered by the leaders in the church. He had previously identified the *yeser ha-ra* (the evil impulse) as a source of evil within a person. Here he identifies a source contributing to the *yeser ha-ra*, which is Satan (*Gehenna*, here rendered "hell," could function as an indirect term referring to Satan, just as "heaven" is frequently an indirect term referring to God [Luke 15:21]).

In the Old Testament the Valley of Hinnom formed part of the boundary between the tribes of Judah and Benjamin (Joshua 15:8). It was also the site of the worship of Canaanite gods such as Ba'al and Molech. In association with these rites, child sacrifices were offered in the valley (2 Kings 23:10). Jeremiah said that this valley would be a place of judgment, calling it the "Valley of Slaughter," because of the many Jews who were killed and then thrown into the valley by the Babylonians (Jeremiah 7:29-34). During the second-temple period this valley became associated with the idea of fiery judgment and eschatological judgment (in the ancient Jewish writings of 1 Enoch 26-27). This caused Gehenna to be associated with the fires of hell, and therefore with hell itself.

In the days of James, the Hinnom Valley was where the residents of Jerusalem stacked all their garbage and filth, which was often burned. James is comparing our tongue to this stinky, smoldering trash dump. There are a dozen references to Gehenna in the New Testament. With the exception of the one in James, all of them are found on the lips of Jesus in the Synoptic Gospels. Here, then, is another link between James and the Jesus tradition.

Following the final judgment, Gehenna is a place of punishment and the destruction of the wicked (Matthew 5:22), body and soul are judged in Gehenna (Matthew 10:28; Mark 9:43-47), and this punishment is eternal (Matthew 25:41, 46). Jesus warns against several sins that might cause one to be condemned to Gehenna, including calling a brother a fool (Matthew 5:22) and giving in to sinful inclinations (Matthew 5:29-30). These two themes are prominent in James—further evidence of the link between James and Jesus.

In short, James 3:6 captures and intensifies the thrust of 3:3-5 that the tongue is capable of great harm (including but not limited to gossip, innuendo, flattery, sarcastic humor, and criticism). James lets us know the tongue has such great potential to do harm because it is full of wickedness. Of course, the wickedness doesn't originate in the mouth. It comes from a place deeper inside us: our hearts. Jesus taught that all of our sins originate there: "For out of the heart come evil thoughts—murder, adultery, sexual immorality, theft, false testimony, slander" (Matthew 15:19). Shakespeare wrote, "what the heart thinks the tongue speaks."

> I heard about a professing Christian who got angry on the job and let loose with some oaths. Embarrassed, he turned to his partner and said, "I don't know why I said that. It really isn't in me." His partner wisely replied, "It had to be in you or it couldn't have come out of you."
>
> —Warren W. Wiersbe, *Be Mature, James*, 106.

Can the tongue be controlled? Well, like diabetes, it can be controlled but not cured. Humanly speaking it's a losing battle—and one you always have to fight. But through Jesus victory can be obtained.

There's something inherent in power that gravitates toward evil (Daniel 7:2-7). Daniel, like James, gives voice to the truth that the powerful often abuse power, just as the tongue often causes hurt. The point of this image is that human institutions possess "authority" because God has delegated that authority to them. However, in our stewardship, that authority has been corrupted by evil—it cannot be trusted, and one day God will strip human institutions of the authority we now use inappropriately. Instead, he will give it to the Son of Man, God's agent, who will establish God's kingdom.

Political power is morally neutral, but easily it's coopted by evil. The Bible therefore argues that the political order, though morally neutral, is inherently weak and easily corrupted by Satan.

James 3:7-8

[7]All kinds of animals, birds, reptiles and sea creatures are being tamed and have been tamed by mankind, [8]but no human being can tame the tongue. It is a restless evil, full of deadly poison.

In juxtaposition to the inability of human beings to control the tongue, James offers the idea that human beings can and have trained many animals. The ancients generally viewed the animal kingdom as symbolic of disorder, but they also prided themselves on their ability to tame nature. Perhaps it would be better to say that the ancients believed that reason governed both nature and human convention, and that when human beings were able to harness nature, it was evidence of the potency of the rational spirit in the universe.

But James also clearly has in mind the biblical account of creation, especially God granting to humankind the right to rule over "the fish in the sea and the birds in the sky, over the livestock, over all the wild animals, and over all the creatures that move along the ground" (Genesis 1:26). James even employs the typical biblical division of the animal world in four classes (Genesis 9:2). This reference to creation calls to mind the recurrent theme of "mature and complete" which carries the nuance of "proper end." God created human beings for a purpose, and this purpose won't be met by following the false teachers.

> He does not say no one can tame the tongue, but no one of [human being]: so that when it is tamed we confess that this is brought about by the pity, the help, and the grace of God.
>
> —Augustine

The image James uses here is of an inadequately caged beast that breaks forth with irrational destructive power. The restless irrationality is akin to the double-mindedness of the tongue. The destructive power is further colored by the description of the tongue as full of deadly poison that trickles long after the words are spoken. Not only is the tongue controlled by irrational destructive powers, but also its arsenal is enhanced by a stock of deadly venom. The image was not unknown to the Hebrews, as Psalm 140:3 says: "They make their tongues as sharp as a serpent's, the poison of vipers is on their lips."

James 3:9

⁹With the tongue we praise our Lord and Father, and with it we curse human beings, who have been made in God's likeness.

Having made the claim that the tongue is untrustworthy and two-faced, almost schizophrenic, James goes on in verse 9 to provide an example from human experience. James avoids the use of metaphor to make this point, preferring instead an image drawn from a church worship service setting. This tongue as the agent of double-minded expressions was known in Judaism (Psalm 62:4b, "With their mouths they bless, but in their hearts they curse.") as we have already seen.

According to James we use the tongue for expressions that are mutually incompatible. As the awareness of the holiness of God developed within Judaism, the Jews devised elliptical ways of speaking of God, one of which was "the Holy One, blessed be He" (also Mark 14:61). James hopes this particularly arresting and poignant example serves as a stern warning concerning the importance of careful supervision over the tongue. The expression "Lord and Father" is used only here in the New Testament.

To this example he adds, "with it we curse human beings, who have been made in God's likeness." The question of cursing is a minor but interesting one in the New

Testament. Jesus cursed the fig tree (Matthew 21:19 also 23:27-28). Paul seems to have been less immune to cursing when the situation seemed to demand strong talk regarding a man found guilty of incest (1 Corinthians 5:5); in at least one case he judged that the condemnation of some was well deserved (Romans 3:8). But these are the exceptions, as the New Testament generally is against cursing. The idea was, obviously, to limit displays of irrational anger. This fits nicely with the general thrust of James' teaching.

It's also clear that the failure to perceive in one another God's image is being considered here. By showing favoritism and by displaying an anti-law spirit that apparently treated the commandment to love one's neighbor as an insignificant act, certain church leaders were actually encouraging a deviant teaching and practice. Failure to recognize that each of us is created in the image of God will eventually allow us to oppress and enslave one another. This is, in fact, a primary reason why the worship of foreign gods was outlawed by God, for the worship of other gods meant not only the rejection of God, but also repudiation of his social and ethical standards.

The church worship service setting further intensifies the importance of the issue. How can worshipers consciously mistreat their fellows, and then expect to worship God in purity? So this verse neatly combines the two deviant practices of the church to which James writes.

James 3:10-12

10Out of the same mouth come praise and cursing. My brothers and sisters, this should not be. 11Can both fresh water and salt water flow from the same spring? 12My brothers and sisters, can a fig tree bear olives, or a grapevine bear figs? Neither can a salt spring produce fresh water.

In verse 10 James is perhaps drawing on Psalm 62:4b,

"With their mouths they bless, but in their hearts they curse." James alters the image to be a falsehood issued by the mouth—a change that perhaps takes place in order to remind his readers of the words of Jesus in Matthew 15:11, "What goes into someone's mouth does not defile them, but what comes out of their mouth, that is what defiles them." Jesus understood actions to be revealing of character, as the saying, "A good tree cannot produce bad fruit" (Matthew 7:18) attests. He also believed our speech to be revealing of character, which is the essential point that James makes here. Our speech comes from the heart. We need to speak graciously always.

In verse 11 James brings in the first of two illustrations from nature that includes a phrase of stock Mediterranean wisdom, rendered in Latin as *a fonte puro pura defluit aqua* ("from a pure spring flows pure water"). He also returns to the world of metaphor. A spring from which issued forth both fresh and salt water was unnatural; in this way James continues to make the point that such speech is irrational.

> If a cup is filled only with good water, it cannot spill even one drop of bitter water, no matter how badly it is jarred.
> —Oswald Chambers

This image of the illogicality of expecting trees and vines to produce fruit not their own is intended to round out the point he has made again and again. Jesus used a similar illustration in Matthew 7:16-20; 12:33-35; and Luke 6:43-45.

James' use of the phrase "my brothers and sisters" (vv.10-11) suggests an admission on his part that he has said some harsh words to his readers, and he is thus restating his affection for them, to recall to their minds the fact that he is one of them, that he has their best interests at heart.

While I was attending a Christian college I was also a part-time youth minister in Compton, California. I liked the church because it was racially integrated, which was unusual in the late 1960s. The youth group was a rainbow of colors, and we all got along well. The new senior pastor called me one day and said I needed to resign and leave the church, but he did not explain why. I thought he and I had gotten along fine even if we did not say much to each other.

I remember feeling dumbfounded and very discouraged as his request came so unexpectedly. I went to my one and only board meeting (at that church) that week to hand in my resignation (as my psych professor had suggested). I knew most of the men in attendance, as I had many of their kids in my youth group. I sat through the entire meeting until the chairman of the board asked in a curious way why I was there. I told him, but he had no idea what I was talking about. The senior minister turned red and said nothing.

I stayed at the church another six months but felt very uncomfortable, as the senior pastor never said a word to me. The senior minister left a couple of years later.

It was not until 30 years later that I received a call from that same senior minster, and he explained the rest of the story. There was an elder on that board who was a very mean older white man with a bad mouth. He did not like that the church was becoming racially integrated and let a few people know it. The minister went on to tell me that this man especially did not like the fact that our youth group was even more racially diverse than the rest of the church. The minister then explained that this racially prejudiced elder told him that if he as a new and young (only about five years older than me) senior pastor (with two babies) did not fire me, this elder would get *him* fired. So he did (asking me for my resignation). At that elder meeting, this one elder would not speak up in front of the other elders. Then the minister also told me that a few months after I had left that potty-mouthed elder's only daughter married a black man, and a few weeks later that elder died of a heart attack. The tongue can do a great deal of damage.

—Les

READ BETWEEN THE LINES

- Is James discouraging people from going into teaching?
- Why do teachers incur a stricter judgment?
- Why does James compare bits in the mouths of horses and a ship's rudder with the tongue?
- How is a forest fire like the tongue?
- What does it mean when he writes the tongue is set on fire by hell (who is behind this?)?
- How can the tongue poison relationships?
- How is praise and cursing coming out of the same mouth similar to fresh and salt water coming from the spring?
- What happens to the fresh water when salt water begins to flow out of the same spring?
- If a fig tree cannot bear olives or a grapevine bear figs, what are we to do about our tongue?
- What is the link between what a person says and their character?

WELCOME TO MY WORLD

- Think of a teacher who made a positive influence on my life, what did they say that caused me to think of them?
- How has my tongue gotten me into trouble?
- How have I been hurt by destructive words?
- When do I find it most difficult to control my tongue?
- What inconsistencies or contradictory words do I see in how I talk to other people compared to how I talk to God?
- There is an old saying, "You are what you eat." What am I allowing into my life and heart that ends up coming out of my mouth?
- What is one thing I would like to change about my speech?

- What have I discovered to be helpful in controlling my tongue?
- How can my tongue bring encouragement and healing?

Two Kinds of Wisdom

James 3:13

¹³Who is wise and understanding among you? Let them show it by their good life, by deeds done in the humility that comes from wisdom.

James here offers us a series of clear contrasts between two kinds of wisdom. This passage is also a fine example of the essential unity of the letter, despite the opinion of many that the letter is an ill-fitting collection of moral teachings.

The early portion of chapter 3 concerned itself with the problem of false teachers and their dangerous teaching by employing the image of the tongue. This "fire" of 3:5-12 is almost certainly the cause of the bitter envy, ambition, and divisions discussed in this present section.

James holds up for praise the wise teacher and the wisdom that comes from God, and contrasts it with the false wisdom offered by his opponents. James also continues here his discussion of the source of the evil within us. In the first chapter James touched upon the presence of the *yeser ha-ra* (inclination to do evil) within us, and in 3:6 he referred to Gehenna, an indirect expression for Satan. In 3:15 James offers a more pointed observation: Some within the church are exhibiting behaviors that are of the devil. This telescopic series of statements concerning the source of evil therefore anchors this passage firmly within the epistle as a whole.

James begins in verse 13 by offering an alternative vision of wisdom, that true wisdom isn't marked by ambition and a desire for status, but rather by humility. Being wise doesn't mean we understand everything that's going on because of our superior knowledge, but that we do the right thing as life comes along.

The chief interpretive problem here is the identification of the "who" that opens the passage. Clearly the teachers who James has opposed are in view. They have given themselves positions of authority as qualified to instruct the Christian community, and in so doing have offered themselves as "wise," just as the false teachers of 1 Corinthians 1:19 laid claim to the mantle of wisdom. To James it's the wisdom of the world and therefore false. But it's also likely that many others in the church are within the field of James' gaze. Certainly there were some, perhaps more than a few, who were captivated by the message of these teachers—a message which spoke to their human desires to attain privilege and status.

The fact that James connects wise (*sophos*) and understanding (*epistemon*) in verse 13 is significant. In Deuteronomy 1:13 and 15 the terms refer to the leaders, but in Deuteronomy 4:6 the terms appearing in tandem refer to the people at large. (In Daniel 5:12 Daniel is described as a man with a "keen mind and knowledge and understanding.") To follow the decrees of God is the hallmark of wisdom. Other nations, the Hebrews are promised, will call them wise if their deeds match the decrees of God. Just as in James, the leaders of Deuteronomy 1:13, 15 must have deeds to match their words.

James next offers a definition of wisdom intended to devastate the position of his opponents. True wisdom, he says, results in humility and good deeds shown in a good life. The noun the NIV translates as "life" is *anastrophe*, better rendered "way of life" or "mode of life." It's used favorably by 1 Peter (1:15; 2:12; 3:1-2, 16). The force of the term indicates that these deeds of humility are embedded in the core of the Christian. True believers radiate such principles and actions.

The worldly pseudo-wisdom of the false teachers has had its corrosive consequences—acts of favoritism within the Christian community and legitimizing actions at odds with the "law of love." The contrast is between the different origins of these two "wisdoms," and between the different actions which follow in sequence.

The phrase *en prauteti sophias* ("the humility that comes from wisdom") is somewhat unwieldy, suggesting that its origin is Hebrew and not Greek. There are parallels in both the Old Testament and the New. Neither Moses (see Numbers 12:1-3) nor Jesus (see Matthew 11:29) were interested in personal popularity or power, neither did they defend themselves, but in humility pointed others to God. In similar fashion the Christian in humility is to do good deeds to the glory of God. This is the spirit of true wisdom.

The late Howard Hendricks, who taught at Dallas Theological Seminary for more than 60 years, told the story of a terrific teacher he met at a Sunday school convention:

A number of us who were speaking there went across the street at noon to get a bite to eat at a hamburger stand. The place was crowded and people were standing in line. An elderly lady was in front of me. I guessed she was about 65—she was 83, I learned later. She wore a convention badge, so I knew she was a conferee. There was a table for four open, so two friends and I invited her to join us. I asked her the obvious question: "Do you teach a Sunday school class?"

"Oh, I certainly do," she said. I visualized a class of senior citizens, but asked her: "What age group do you teach?"

"I teach a class of junior high boys."

"Junior high boys! How many boys do you have?"

"Thirteen," she said sweetly.

"Tremendous! I suppose you come from a rather large church."

"No, sir, it's very small," she said. "We have about 55 in Sunday school."

Hardly daring to go on, I said, "What brings you to this Sunday school convention?"

"I'm on a pension—my husband died a number of years ago," she replied, "and, frankly, this is the first time a convention has come close enough to my home so I could afford to attend. I bought a Greyhound ticket and rode all night to get here this morning and attend two workshops. I want to learn something that will make me a better teacher."

Hendricks went on to add, "I heard a sequel to this story some time later. A doctor told me there are 84 young men in or moving toward the Christian ministry as a result of this woman's influence."

As Howard Hendricks would say, "May her tribe increase!"

—Taken from a taped message given by Dr. Howard Hendricks at College Church in Wheaton, Ill.

James 3:14

¹⁴But if you harbor bitter envy and selfish ambition in your hearts, do not boast about it or deny the truth.

Verse 14 presents a contrasting picture: a bitter and selfish person. The term which the NIV translates as "bitter envy" is *zelon pikron. Zelon* is derived from *zelos*, often translated into English as "zeal." It can bear a negative nuance (see Romans 13:13; 2 Corinthians 12:20; Galatians 5:20), often depicting someone overblown with an inappropriate sense of devotion to God. Paul describes his own past as marked by a zeal for God in persecuting the church (Philippians 3:6; see also Romans 10:2, where Paul describes the Israelites as, "zealous for God, but their zeal is not based upon knowledge").

If your words are bitter, it's because your heart is bitter. Jesus tells us in Matthew 12:34, "For the mouth speaks what the heart is full of." Bitter words come from a bitter heart.

The term "zeal" can also be used in the positive sense (See 1 Kings 19:10, 14; John 2:17; 2 Corinthians 7:7; and especially 2 Corinthians 11:2 where Paul speaks of "godly jealousy") but of course any zeal has the potential for great destruction if turned. In this case it appears that zeal for self-interest has resulted in attitudes of envy and desire that are so overgrown they engulf whatever better judgment may have been present.

The term the NIV translates as "selfish ambition" is *eritheia*. Some argue that it is derived from *eris*, which can mean "discord." However, others point out that the word is rare outside the New Testament; its only appearance prior to the New Testament is by Aristotle, who uses it to mean the self-seeking pursuit of political power by unjust means. This more precise rendering makes sense here.

Paul's use of *eris* appears in the lists of vices (2 Corinthians 12:20; Galatians 5:20) and together with *zelos* is used to describe leaders who cause discord by claiming superior wisdom and gathering to themselves followers while they charge the others in the church with a lack of spirituality. Discord has come to the Christian community as a result of teachers who have appealed to the desire for self-seeking status in the Roman world, and they have usurped the spiritual offices of the church in order to teach and propagate this very worldly philosophy.

To understand James' urging these teachers and their followers to refrain from "boast[ing] about it," we must first understand to what the "it" refers. Most likely it refers to the wisdom they claim. So we might translate this: "Do not boast about your worldly wisdom, because to do so is only to deny the truth even more clearly." What the teachers falsely call "wisdom" is in fact the poisonous work of the *yeser ha-ra* in human hearts. There is a heavenly truth, a truth they deny, a truth which is the polar opposite of the "truth" they disseminate.

James 3:15

15Such "wisdom" does not come down from heaven but is earthly, unspiritual, demonic.

Significantly in verse 15 James does not label "wisdom" what his opponents advocate as wisdom, preferring to refer to it in veiled fashion. Their "wisdom" is not from God, which can be had simply by asking (1:5). In saying this James makes a clear argument that the wisdom of these teachers is not neutral or trivial.

He does this by arranging the sources of this "wisdom" in an escalating buildup of wickedness. The first is *epigeios*, or earthbound. Here the image of the world, as elsewhere in James, is called upon to play a negative role. "Earthly" is contrasted with wisdom "from above" and by definition is less pure and inferior, and in this instance refers to the forces arrayed against God. James also intends to remind his readers that the world is at odds with God. He is saying "do not fool yourself into thinking that this attitude is in concert with God, for such is a lie." This "wisdom" is self-centered and shallow.

Next, this wisdom is *psychikos*, or "unspiritual." This is a fairly unusual word, found in only four other locations in the New Testament (1 Corinthians 2:14; 15:44, 46; Jude 19). Paul uses the term to describe the "natural man," as it is drawn from Genesis 2:7 where God breathes life into Adam and he becomes a living *psyche*. In this regard it can denote the unrealized potential to respond positively to God. *Psychikos* was sometimes used by dissenting groups to describe their opponents. The term was therefore meant to denote beings possessing merely life without the touch of the Spirit of God.

Such persons are responsive only to natural stimuli. The false teachers had accused James of this, and of a lack of wisdom. Deftly James causes this accusation to turn in their hands. He points out that the activity of the false teachers, this self-righteous name-calling, is in fact a facade which is the result of the very "natural," "base" and "unspiritual" desire for personal status and prestige.

Such "wisdom" is, worst of all, demonic in origin. This

term, *daimoniodes*, is quite rare, as it does not appear elsewhere in Scripture, and apparently is not to be found in Greek literature before James. There are two options as to its meaning:

1. This teaching and its derivative behavior is instigated by demons and the unwholesome spiritual world;
2. The behavior depicted here is similar to that of the demons.

There is no good reason to suppose that James did not have the first in mind.

James 3:16

16For where you have envy and selfish ambition, there you find disorder and every evil practice.

In verse 16 James argues from the perspective of the practical. The wisdom of his opponents rooted in "envy and selfish ambition," has done nothing to strengthen the body, but rather has served only to bring selfish discord. In case his readers are not yet convinced, James points out that such tumult and division could not possibly be the result of true wisdom, because true wisdom is heavenly. True wisdom can also bring discord, because true wisdom is faithful to the heavenly standard. True wisdom does not confuse issues of primary allegiance with those of secondary or tertiary character.

While the speech of Jesus is at times overstated to make a point (e.g., "If anyone comes to me and does not hate father and mother...such a person cannot be my disciple"— Luke 14:26), the point is clear. Jesus demands our primary allegiance. True wisdom does not tolerate the discord which results from selfish personal interest. The source of such tumult and mean-spirited talk is Satan.

The word the NIV renders with "disorder" is *akatastasia*—the same word used in 1:8 for the unstable, double-minded person. Here, as in 3:8, the scenario is not about an individual, but the Christian community. This teaching has not added to the church but instead has caused the church to seriously question its direction—even its heart and soul.

James 3:17

17But the wisdom that comes from heaven is first of all pure; then peace-loving, considerate, submissive, full of mercy and good fruit, impartial and sincere.

James goes on, then, to list in verse 17 what he considers being among the most important results of heavenly wisdom. James does so in a list of characteristics or virtues that he strings together like pearls, similar to those given by Paul in his list of "the fruits of the spirit" (Galatians 5:22-23).

First of all, this wisdom is marked by purity. Purity is listed first because in many ways it is the most important, paving the way for the others. The Greek term for "pure" is *hagne*, which is fairly unique (see also 1 John 3:3 and Philippians 4:8). It signifies the absence of the spiritual, ethical, and behavioral imperfections which are a part of the double-minded person.

The concept is found in the Old Testament, usually in connection with the character of God. God's words are pure (Psalm 12:6); and the ways of the righteous are pure, not bent (Proverbs 21:8) because the lives of the righteous mirror God's character. Here then is another reference to the rightful "end" or "purpose" of humankind. A person marked by purity partakes of the character of God, following after God with "unmixed motives." Jesus said in Matthew 5:8, "Blessed are the pure in heart, for they will see God."

James has arranged the remaining seven virtues so that the first four in the Greek begin with the *e* sound and the last two with a nice *a* sound: peace-loving (*eirenike*), considerate (*epieikes*), submissive (*eupeithes*), full of mercy (*meste eleous*), good fruit (*karpon agathon*), impartial (*adiakritos*), and sincere (*anupokritos*). Such wisdom also creates a peace-making spirit. This is of particular importance given the problem of discord in the church.

"Peace-loving" gathers together a number of distinct ideas that are at work in this passage, as the wisdom of God leads to the peace and wholeness God desires of and for us.

> **This does not suggest, as some may hear it, an attitude of peace by abdication—like the couple who had just celebrated their fiftieth wedding anniversary. Someone asked the gentleman the secret of their marital bliss. "Well," the old man drawled, "the wife and I had this agreement when we first got married. It went like this: When she was bothered about somethin', she'd jus' tell me and git it off her chest. And if I was mad at her about somethin', I was able to take a long walk. I s'ppose you could attribute our happy marriage to the fact that I have largely led an outdoor life."**
>
> **—R. Kent Hughes, *James: Faith That Works*, 157-158.**

There are proper times to "take a walk," but James is not recommending a peace that depends on walking away from conflict. Nor is James talking about a "peace at any price" that keeps us on the fence, agreeing with whomever we might be talking to at the moment.

In the Old Testament "peace" (*shalom*) means, "to be whole, to be healthy, to be complete." *Shalom* was employed in a variety of ways. The daily greeting in Israel was *shalom alekem* ("peace be upon you"), a blessing and greeting meaning "may you be well." *Shalom* is used of prosperity (Psalm 73:3); physical health (Psalm 38:3); and salvation (Isaiah 43:7). *Shalom* can be used in connection with death. The promise to Abraham is, "You, however, will go down to your fathers in peace and be buried at a good old age." *Shalom* is also connected to the covenant. In Numbers 25:12 the Lord says to Moses, "I am making my covenant of peace..." The Old Testament also contrasts peace with warfare.

True wholeness, true peace, is intimately linked with the character of God. This idea is present in Psalm 34:14 where the psalmist says, "Turn from evil and do good, seek peace and pursue it." In Psalm 34 peace is linked to the very core of God's character, and it must be pursued. Peace has a future orientation as well. The "Prince of Peace" is the agent of God who brings God's justice and truth and peace. Jesus said in Matthew 5:9, "Blessed are the peacemakers, for they will be called children of God."

"Considerate" is usually associated with justice, especially with the administration of justice, and suggests a person who does not abuse a position of power, but remains calm and sober and true to the highest ideals of such a position. This is the person who makes allowances for the weakness and ignorance of others. (In 1 Timothy 3:3, Paul uses it to describe the ideal behavior of church leaders.)

"Submissive" does not indicate a person without convictions, or one easily swayed. Rather it conjures the image of a sober, thinking, and intuitive person who recognizes the truth when heard, and willingly receives such instruction. This person has a teachable open spirit. This person can disagree without being disagreeable. Together these two virtues denote someone who is both gentle and reasonable, whether in a position of authority or subservience.

"Full of mercy" and "Good fruits" imply looking upon others with compassion when they deserve punishment. However, it's not just compassion which results in pity and sympathy; it's compassion in *action*. Mercy is showing kindness and benevolence. *Good fruits* means bountiful blessings to others. James has told us that true religion is evidenced by acts of kindness (1:27), and that faith is seen in deeds of charity (2:15-18).

"Impartial" is a word of great rarity found only here in the New Testament. But it's the opposite of "double-minded," a word James has used frequently. Wisdom possesses a singularity of purpose in its trust in God. It does not vacillate—it is objective, impartial, and fair.

"Sincere" is the final word and a fine capstone to the list, as it also can mean "without hypocrisy." This is someone who does not wear a false mask. The essence of hypocrisy is shiftiness, instability, unpredictability. There is no pretense in a sincere person. Paul's first command in Romans 12:9 is "love must be sincere."

Some suggest the word "sincere" came from the Latin words *sine cera*, which mean "without wax." The phrase was in response to people who would hide the cracks in cheap pottery with wax in order to pass the pottery off as being worth more than it actually was. Quality products were often stamped with the words *sine cera* to show it had not been doctored. It would be similar to those products today that are stamped, "all natural" or "100% pure." Paul is telling us to love in a way that is pure and genuine.

James 3:18

18Peacemakers who sow in peace reap a harvest of righteousness.

Taken as a whole the virtues are meant to counteract the divisive and party spirit, and to prompt openness to God's leading, so that even the teachers James opposes might see the light.

In his final comment James not surprisingly focuses upon peace, given the discord in the church. In Matthew 5:9 Jesus promises that the peacemakers will be blessed. Their reward will be to see a right relationship between God and people.

When James encourages his readers to be "peacemakers

who sow in peace (and who) reap a harvest of righteousness," it is again this complex idea of *shalom* to which he refers. Justice, righteousness, and peace are central to the character of God. To develop such character in ourselves and within the Christian community has been a frequent theme throughout the course of this letter.

Righteousness and peace are regularly linked in the Old Testament (Psalm 85:10; Isaiah 32:17). The phrase "harvest of righteousness" is somewhat difficult. Sophie Laws insightfully argues that the "harvest of righteousness" is in fact wisdom. If she is correct, then the argument of James is:

- where there is divisiveness there is no wisdom because wisdom is peaceable;
- therefore the peacemakers are the ones who possess wisdom;
- and the ones who create tumult and discord do not possess wisdom, however much they protest to the opposite.

The opponents of James have claimed, either explicitly or implicitly, to possess a superior wisdom. By defining wisdom in biblical terms James has shown his opponents to be spreaders of a highly corrosive brew of worldly wisdom and deficient teaching. In short, he has shown them to be *psychikoi* (worldly minded, not having the spirit), the very charge they leveled at James.

The church can never have peace by sweeping sins under the rug and pretending they are not there. Peace which leads to righteousness is peace which steadfastly refuses to let go of its standards: justice, righteousness, and the wisdom of God. Peace bought at their sacrifice is not biblical peace.

READ BETWEEN THE LINES

- What does it mean to be "wise"?
- What does heavenly wisdom produce?

- What does worldly wisdom produce?
- Why would someone boast about envy and selfish ambition?
- What does it mean to "sow in peace"?
- How does a wise person resolve clashes?

WELCOME TO MY WORLD

- What can I do to stimulate genuine peace within my circle of acquaintances?
- How has my selfishness and envy gotten me in trouble in the past?
- Where is it most difficult for me to show the kind of wisdom described in verse 17?
- Which of the characteristics in verse 17 am I strong in and which ones am I weak in?
- Do I rejoice when others succeed or do I envy and criticize them?
- How can I nurture (develop) these qualities?
- Is James suggesting I become a doormat by avoiding conflict at all costs, always giving in when opposed? Explain.

Submit Yourselves to God

There are a number of ties between this passage and those which have come before, in spite of a variety of commentators who tell us otherwise. The section just completed (3:13-18) was concerned with true wisdom which issues forth in peace, and false wisdom which results in disorder and strife. Here James again discusses disorder (4:2) that results from this same false wisdom, the ultimate source of which is the devil (4:7).

James 4:1-10 continues the record of the increasing steps in the progress of evil. In 1:14 the evil desire (*yeser-ha-ra*) was introduced. In 3:6 James pronounced that Gehenna was the cause of the fire of the tongue. In 3:15 the origin of the "wisdom" of the world was identified as demonic. Here in 4:7 Christians are told to resist the devil. The pride of 4:6 is linked to the boasting of 3:14; the selfish ambition of 3:14 is linked to the human heart which must be cleansed in 4:8. Finally, the statement that "friendship with the world means enmity against God" in 4:4 refers to the passionate desire of some in the community to seek status and prestige as their surrounding culture defines it. In the pursuit of this they showed favoritism and displayed an unwillingness to understand the law of love, thereby showing themselves opposed to God.

In this passage James once again points out the two choices placed before the church. James has just finished laying before our eyes the source, origin, and results of the ways of earth and the ways of heaven. He provides a concrete example of the growth of sin that he offered in the first chapter. The seriousness of the matter is confirmed in the harsh vocabulary arranged by James: They "kill" (4:2); they are an "adulterous people" (4:4) whose actions make them "enemies of God" (4:4); they are "sinners" (4:8). The choice James sets before them is simple: Earthly wisdom or heavenly wisdom, self-interest or the law of love, self-exaltation or exaltation at the hand of God.

James 4:1-10 is composed of three sections. The first two offer diagnoses of the problems rampant in the church. The third offers a solution. In the first section (4:1-3) James chastises his readers for their prayers, for these are marked by anger and selfish desire, not by an attitude of trust in God. In the second section (4:4-6) James points out that there are substantial and significant differences between the values of the Roman Empire and a life lived according to God's desires. A choice must be made: No one can satisfy the demands of both. In the final section (4:7-10) James offers his solution to the various problems besetting the church as he issues a call to repentance.

James 4:1

¹What causes fights and quarrels among you? Don't they come from your desires that battle within you?

James in verse 1 asks a question knowing full well the answer.

James compares the effects of the tongue under the influence of false wisdom with rather serious parallels: Fights (*polemoi*) and quarrels (*machai*). The term *machai* is reserved for fights without weapons; these battles can be physical or verbal. The church is plagued by jealousy, selfish ambition, slander, anger, a willingness to depart from received teaching, and a host of other ills that follow the pattern of its culture.

As Swindoll points out, "we should expect the world, with its back to God and devoid of His Word and Spirit, to be characterized by fighting. People fight in business, in politics, in religion, in education, in marriage, in sports. But sad to say, believers also fight in church." There are fights over doctrinal issues, power struggles, and insignificant grievances. The fact that James refers to no specific dispute might signal to us a situation so rife with tensions that the church was at a standstill. In any event, the conflict is clearly within the Christian community, as this is certainly the meaning of *en umin* (among you).

The picture then is as follows: Certain teachers had won a following by offering a philosophy which encouraged the pursuit of status as taught by society. This allowed a false belief to germinate and flourish that all of the old prejudices could exist and thrive within the church. For this reason some were showing favoritism, and others were exploiting the poor. Arrayed against these were some loyal to the gospel who correctly understood the threat. The members of this group reacted in various ways to those following the teachers of false wisdom—some wanting peace at any price, others advocating a fight for the soul of the church—and there followed a whole catalogue of numerous tensions and disputes within the community.

In the second part of verse 1, James wisely points out that just as there are mixed within each of us as individual's motives and emotions wholesome and unwholesome, so within the Christian community there is a wide variety of impulses. James says these disputes come from the desires (*hedone*) within them. This Greek word is the source of our English word *hedonism*; the philosophy that pleasure is the main goal of life.

The rabbis believed that the impulses, the *yeser*, had their seats in various organs or "members" of the human body; therefore the members of the body were "at war" with one another, pulled one way by conscience (good *yeser*), then another way by selfish desire (selfish *yeser*).

The image is found elsewhere in the New Testament: 1 Peter 2:11 speaks of "sinful desires" which "war against your soul." In Romans 7:22-23 Paul speaks of the two "laws" within him, "For in my inner being I delight in God's law; but I see another law at work in in me, waging war...and making me a prisoner of the law of sin at work within me."

Such passions—or more properly, the decision to cultivate rather than control evil passions—have contributed to the problems within the church. These evil passions (e.g., unrestrained desire for power and authority, a desire for popularity within the eyes of the powerful, etc.) within the church create double-mindedness. The members of the congregation are pushed this way and that, first by their conscience, then by the evil impulse.

James 4:2-3

2You desire but do not have, so you kill. You covet but you cannot get what you want, so you quarrel and fight. You do not have because you do not ask God. 3When you ask, you do not receive, because you ask with wrong motives, that you may spend what you get on your pleasures.

In verse 2a James punctuates his message by noting that unrestrained desire can never be fulfilled: "You kill. You covet, but you cannot get what you want" refers to present difficulties. Several commentators have attempted to see "murder" (*phoneuete*) as metaphorical (e.g., murder in our hearts and with our lips). For Jesus, the commandment against murdering applied equally to verbal assassination as to physical killing (Matthew 5:21-22; 1 John 3:15).

The term can be understood literally (see King David's murder of Uriah the Hittite in 2 Samuel 11:1-27), even if we do not know the particulars. We see this in the news, in segments featuring a person who ends up murdering the one he says he loves. It's significant that James adds the reason for this killing is covetousness (envy). James is explaining that to choose the path of violence is to place oneself within a vicious cycle of retribution. Only the peace offered by God can stop such a tragic web of circumstances. Envy sheepishly wants what someone else possesses. Swindoll offers the following practical advice on the cure for envy:

> What's the cure? *Contentment.* Feeling comfortable and secure with who you are and where you are. Not having to "be better" or "go further" or "own more" or "prove to the world" or "reach the top." Contentment means surrendering your frustrated hopes and missed goals to God, who alone "makes poor and rich; He brings low, He also exalts" (1 Samuel 2:7). Having some struggles with envy? Eating your heart out because somebody's a step or two ahead of you in the race and gaining momentum? *Relax.* You are *you*—not him or her! And you're responsible to do the best you can with what you've got for as long as you're able.
>
> —Swindoll, *Insights on James, 1 and 2 Peter*, 93.

The last part of verse 2 contains a theme we have already seen (1:5). What James' readers want is not simply status, but rather what they hope status will bring to them: a sense of wholeness, of joy, of peace. James says they do not have what they seek because they have been searching for it in alleys that are blind and in fields that are infertile. They should ask God, who gives wisdom (1:5), and this is a wisdom that results in wholeness and peace.

In Matthew 7:7: "Ask and it will be given to you; seek and you will find; knock and the door will be opened to you." Jesus gave an unconditional promise that prayer would be answered, and James makes explicit what Jesus left implicit. You do not receive because you ask God not for wisdom, but for selfish pleasures that by definition are not in the interests of the Christian community. The significant point is that the readers of James ask with the wrong motives, and therefore for the wrong things.

> When John Ward, a member of the British Parliament, died, a prayer was found among his papers:
>
> "O Lord, Thou knowest that I have nine estates in the City of London, and likewise that I have lately purchased an estate in the county of Essex. I beseech Thee to preserve the two counties of Middlesex and Essex from fires and earthquakes and as I have a mortgage in Hertfdordshire, I beg of Thee likewise to have an eye of compassion on that county. As for the rest of the counties, Thou mayest deal with them as Thou art pleased."
>
> —John Blanchard, *Truth for Life*, 222-223.

James is not describing a "name it and claim it" theology. James warns against pleasure-motivated prayers. The prayers were not answered positively because, in part, the prayers were arrogant—the presumption being that the one praying knew what was best. God's wisdom often is at odds with our presumed wisdom, and this was the case here. Unfortunately patience and a willingness to be molded by God were evidently absent. We need to be praying for things that bring glory to God.

James 4:4

⁴You adulterous people, don't you know that friendship with the world means enmity against God? Therefore, anyone who chooses to be a friend of the world becomes an enemy of God.

In verse 4 James adopts the mantle of elder and offers a rebuke as to errant children. By designating them "adulterous" he recalls a frequent Old Testament rebuke (see the premise of Hosea and Jeremiah 3:7-10) and offers an echo of the teaching of Jesus in Matthew 12:39. They are adulterous because they are cheating on God. Their attention, affection, and allegiance are not toward God and his people, but toward themselves and the world. James is here chastising them and trying to shame them by reminding them of their commitment to the faith.

James' reference to friendship with the world closely parallels a phrase employed by Paul in 2 Timothy 3:4 ("lovers of pleasure rather than lovers of God") and by John in 1 John 2:15 ("Do not love the world or anything in the world. If anyone loves the world, love for the Father is not in him"). The "world" here refers to the forces and elements opposed to God, or more precisely the whole complex of human institutions, values, and traditions that knowingly or unwittingly are arrayed against God.

Some who choose friendship with the world do so with the full knowledge that this constitutes hostility with God. Yet they continue to maintain an appearance of some relationship with the Christian community. Perhaps James suspects this of the teachers he opposes. Others choose friendship with the world without realizing that this means hostility with God. This is probably James' chief point, for the phrase "adulterous people" is always used in Scripture regarding those who assume they're in a covenant relationship with God. Why else would James seek to win them back by argument and then rebuke?

Like the prophets of old he wants his readers and listeners to wake up, rub the sleep from their eyes, look in the mirror (1:23), and see themselves as they really are. What has appeared to them to be sound teaching and practice is actually a departure from those principles and beliefs. It amounts to the worship of a false god. There is no middle ground where one might stand and remain unsullied (1:27). To continue to follow this false teaching is no small thing—it is to join hands with evil. They haven't sensed the dire straits in which they stand, and James sounds for them the warning bell.

James 4:5-6

⁵Or do you think Scripture says without reason that he jealously longs for the spirit he has caused to dwell in us? ⁶But he gives us more grace. That is why Scripture says: "God opposes the proud but shows favor to the humble."

Verse 5 presents at least two well-known problems of translation and interpretation. First, what Scripture does James have in mind? There is no Old Testament verse or passage to correspond to the quotation. It's possible that we have here a loose paraphrase or summary of many Old Testament passages (Exodus 20:5, 34:14; Zechariah 8:2, etc.) that speak of the jealousy of God when the worship and ultimate allegiance on the part of human beings is in view. James' point is that God desires his Spirit to reside in us—or "abide" in us, to use John's term (John 14:17, 23).

This leads us to the second problem: What is the subject and what is the object of the verb "longs for" (*epipothei*)? Other renderings are possible and grammatically defensible ("Out of jealousy he longs for the Spirit that he made to live in us" or "The Holy Spirit which he sent to live in us desires us for himself alone"). In any case God desires with all of his heart for us to come home, to dwell with and in him, and for us to ask for his wisdom. Instead we follow the wisdom of the world, whether knowingly or unwittingly, and by following that errant path we can never achieve what truly we seek.

In verse 6 James holds out a lifeline to those who have apparently been ignorant of the gravity of their situation. God's grace, he says, is still available in abundance for them.

God's demands can be harsh, but he always provides the means to follow him. This holds true even in the case of those active in cultivating a friendship with the world. The Apostle John also brings up this truth writing in John 1:16, "Out of his fullness we have all received grace in place of grace already given." Grace and more grace, grace heaped upon grace.

The Scripture that James quotes in verse 6 is Proverbs 3:34: "He mocks proud mockers but shows favor to the humble and oppressed." The writer uses this verse to make it clear that God opposes the proud because they seem to have little interest in anyone but themselves, often exploiting the poor; and that God grants grace (favor) to the poor and needy because they trust in God, having no other recourse (1:6, 12; 2:5; 5:8). In James' situation the proud and arrogant have already shown their stripes: They have demonstrated favoritism based upon wealth and status as the Roman world encouraged, and they have therefore unveiled themselves as the friends of that world and antagonistic to God.

A problem in our churches today is that we have too many celebrities and too few servants. It's not easy to turn from self-absorbed pride and humble ourselves in front of God. But if we do, we'll find an overabundance of God's grace ready to be poured out on us. As Paul wrote in Romans 5:20, "But where sin increased, grace increased all the more." Humility is not a weakness. As God gives us more grace, we realize that this world's seductive attractions are only cheap imitations for what God has to offer.

> **"I do not at all understand the mystery of grace—only that it meets us where we are and does not leave us where it found us."**
>
> **—Anne Lamott, *Traveling Mercies: Some Thoughts on Faith*, 143.**

James 4:7

⁷Submit yourselves, then, to God. Resist the devil, and he will flee from you.

Verse 7 opens a series of ten imperatives, or commands, built on the foundation laid in verse 6. These commands comprise James' recipe for strengthening humility before God. "Submit" (*hypotasso*) is normally used in reference to human authority, but the point is clear and the alternatives stark: You may think you have been serving God, but you have not. Change, then, by submitting to God. The idea of submission carries with it the thought of repentance that consists of not only a change of direction, but also a humble and contrite spirit. If this path is chosen, the response of God is forgiveness and grace, as James has just reminded us in verse 6. James then expands these points.

The first component of submission to God is to "resist the devil." In the Bible, the names "Satan" and "devil" identify the same evil being (Revelation 20:2). James flatly claims that Satan is the ultimate source of the evil desire. Perhaps James has employed an elaborate escalating technique (the *yeser ha-ra* in 1:14; Gehenna in 3:6; the demonic in 3:15; the devil here) in order to mirror the craftiness of Satan himself. The idea that the devil can be resisted is known in both Jewish and Christian thought. For example, the discussion of the armor of God in Ephesians 6 includes the idea that against the powers and the spiritual forces of evil Christians can "stand their ground" when properly prepared. 1 Peter 5:9 also commands Christians to "resist" the devil. Satan has an impressive arsenal of weapons and is deadly deceptive. However, Satan can be resisted, primarily because he is weaker than God.

Within the theology of the New Testament the power of Satan is severely curtailed at the crucifixion and resurrection, and it is quite possible that James has this in mind.

The promise here is that with resistance, the devil will flee. Certainly the resistance of Jesus in the wilderness put Satan to flight, at least for a time (Luke 4:13).

James 4:8

⁸Come near to God and he will come near to you. Wash your hands, you sinners, and purify your hearts, you double-minded.

The parallel to "resist the devil" is "come near to God." As Martin wisely points out, coming to God in this passage is an act of contrition, not one of conversion. This involves the renunciation of all the practices and teachings James has catalogued up to this point in the letter.

In the old system God was separated from the people in the Holy of Holies, in the temple, by a thick curtain. But Christ provided a way through the curtain so that we can approach God without fear. With the phrase "Come near" James taps into the language of eschatology, in which the phrase means "has arrived." When in Mark 1:15 Jesus says, "The kingdom of God has come near," he means that with his activity the kingdom of God has begun to arrive. He does not mean that it is on its way.

The phrase is also used relative to sacrifice. To "come near to present the food offerings" (Leviticus 21:21) means being so close to the altar that a sacrifice may be offered upon it. To "come near to God" then, is more than simply to resolve to improve one's spiritual life. It is to fully enter the presence of God, to reside there, to be comfortable there, and to be at home there. James uses this imagery because he wishes to remind his readers of God's longing to know them. We are to "abide" in the presence of God, and God to "abide" or "dwell" in us, as John's Gospel puts it (John 14:17, 23; 17:21).

> "Draw near to God and he will draw near to you." That is astonishing! God is ready and waiting. He longs to establish a friendship with you, a friendship deeper, stronger and more satisfying than you can ever imagine. This, too, will take time, as any friendship worthy of the name will do. But what could be more worthwhile? If even a few more people were prepared to take these promises seriously, think what a difference it would make to the world, never mind the church.
>
> —N. T. Wright, *The Early Christian Letters for Everyone*, 29.

James has already carefully laid the groundwork concerning purity and evil in chapter 1. Then in chapters 2 and 3 he became rather specific. Now, having established this portrait of evil he next commands renunciation of evil while holding out the promise of gracious forgiveness. This he states in typically Jewish terms of washing and purity. The call of James is to a reorientation to God and his purposes in our world, purposes that touch the social, cultural, and economic juggernauts with which human beings must reckon.

The linkage of "hand" and "heart" in verse 8 is typically Jewish. The Psalms, for instance, frequently speak of the connection between inner disposition and outward acts (Psalms 24:4; 73:13). Jewish priests went through a ceremonial procedure before they offered sacrifices. The tradition was symbolic of the cleansing and purification we need to have accomplished in our own hearts when we enter God's presence. James is telling us to confess our sins so that the condition of our heart is acceptable before the Lord. Psalm 24:3-4, "Who may ascend the mountain of the LORD? Who may stand in his holy place? The one who has clean hands and a pure heart..."

The Life Application Bible Commentary suggests a

connection between washing and submission using the Lord's Supper, where Jesus washed his disciples' feet. They had to submit to his serving them, which Peter found difficult to do (John 13:3-10).

"Sinners" is an interesting choice, as it was precisely these people with whom Jesus associated, much to the consternation of the religious authorities (Matthew 9:10-13). James has used earlier the word "double-minded" to describe the unstable who doubt God (1:8). Here it refers to those who try to live in two natures: one of the world and one of God. This sort of double allegiance is not possible. "Purity of heart" implies single-mindedness.

James says that sin has the power to spring up within us, intertwine itself in the stuff of our lives, and finally to cause death. He tells it like it is, and he wants us to understand the origin, progress, deceptive powers, and eternal consequences of sin.

James 4:9-10

⁹Grieve, mourn and wail. Change your laughter to mourning and your joy to gloom. ¹⁰Humble yourselves before the Lord, and he will lift you up.

The verb which opens verse 9, "grieve" is a common one in the Prophets (Jeremiah 4:8; Joel 2:12-13). James is not opposed to having fun. He is not saying we are to live a life of gloom and doom. He's not telling us we should never smile or laugh. James is not a killjoy, wanting Christians to walk around with long faces and somber expressions. Haven't we all met Christians who seem like they have been baptized in vinegar?

James is referring to scornful laughter that refuses to take sin seriously. There is a time to mourn over our sin. It wasn't until the prodigal son got home and repented that he celebrated; there is no doubt that he shed many tears on the way.

George Guthrie and Douglas Moo have explained that the key to understanding this exhortation is to recognize that "laughter" is often associated with the "fool" in biblical wisdom. This is referring to the person who disrespects the Lord and any moral standards, overrunning in sinful behavior and mocking any idea of judgment to come (Proverbs 10:23; Ecclesiastes 7:6). Jesus reflects the same tradition when he said, "Woe to you who laugh now, for you will mourn and weep" (Luke 6:25b).

The idea of changing laughter to mourning was used in Amos 8:10 to spark a sudden awareness of guilt and repentance. By such signs the Prophets warned of sudden catastrophe which the people had brought upon themselves by their indifference to the poor and therefore to God as well.

In urging grief and a shift from laughter to mourning and joy to gloom James reminds his readers that the false paths they thought would lead to true laughter and joy are dead ends and need to be abandoned. This abandonment must carry with it recognition that the pursuit of these old false paths has not only grieved God, but endangered the Christian community and harmed many of their sisters and brothers. The recognition of such hurt carries with it an awareness of guilt and responsibility that aren't appropriately mixed with laughter and joy.

The verb that begins verse 10, "humble yourselves" (*tapeinoo*) speaks not only of contrition and repentance, but points to the penitent being in the presence of the Lord. By employing this term both here and in verse 6, James has offered a clear stylistic clue to the unity of the passage. This is opposed to the attitude of reckless arrogant indifference to God which characterized the instruction and practice of the false teachers. Humbling ourselves means recognizing our worth comes from God alone.

> Sometimes we hear a believer pray, "O Lord, humble me!" That is a dangerous thing to pray. Far better that we humble ourselves before God, confess our sins, weep over them, and turn from them.
>
> —Warren W. Wiersbe, *Be Mature, James*, 133.

The promise of forgiveness is that God will then "lift you up" (*hypsoo*). This verb normally carries a metaphorical sense. In the Gospel of John the verb bears a literal sense (John 12:32, "And I, when I am lifted up from the earth, will draw all people to myself").

Those who followed the false teachers desired wholeness and joy. James points out that in their true form these things can only be found through humility before God.

READ BETWEEN THE LINES

- Where do fights and quarrels come from?
- How can a Christian pray to God wrongly?
- Is all pleasure wrong?
- What does it mean to have a "friendship with the world"?
- What does it mean to be an adulterous people?
- Why is it impossible to be friends with the world and with God?
- What are some worldly cultural values that seem opposed to God's values?
- Is jealousy always inappropriate?
- Describe grace.
- How does a person resist the devil?
- How does a person come near to God?
- What does it mean for sinners to wash their hands?
- Are we never to laugh or be joyful?
- What does it mean "God will lift you up"?

WELCOME TO MY WORLD

- What causes fights and quarrels with my fellow Christians?
- Why should this not be? What kind of a witness is this to the world?
- How do I usually respond when I don't get what I desire?
- How have I double-crossed God?
- What evidence do I see in my life that resembles friendship with the world?
- How can I keep from being crushed by the world's values?
- What are two areas in my life where I need to resist the devil?
- What should I do when I don't feel close to God? What steps can I take?

Judging Today

Having issued a call to repentance and forgiveness, here James begins a short section in which he discusses unwholesome speech in the form of name-calling and the spreading of lies. James counters this by showing how such behavior repeals the law of loving one's neighbor.

What binds this passage together with those before is the power of the tongue, here understood primarily in the individual sense. If unchecked it is the instrument used to slander others.

James 4:11

¹¹Brothers and sisters, do not slander one another. Anyone who speaks against a brother or sister or judges them speaks against the law and judges it. When you judge the law, you are not keeping it, but sitting in judgment on it.

In verse 11 James uses the phrase "brothers and sisters," tying himself to the church to which he writes. The verb the NIV renders as "slander" is *katalaleo*, and it means "to speak ill of, to talk down to." Slander moves beyond gossip. Slander can involve making an intentionally false statement about someone for the express purpose of damaging his or her reputation. James has in mind harsh criticism and condemnation. Such verbal attacks were among the "quarrels and fights" in view earlier (4:1-2).

There is no shortage of similar material in either the Old or New Testaments. In the Old Testament parallels can be found in the Pentateuch (Leviticus 19:16, "Do not go about spreading slander among your people."), the Psalms (Psalm 101:5, "Whoever slanders their neighbor in secret, I will put to silence."), and the wisdom tradition (Proverbs 10:18, "Whoever conceals hatred with lying lips and spreads slander is a fool."). In the New Testament the term appears in several of the lists of vices (Romans 1:30; 2 Corinthians 12:20).

But the clear reason for not slandering is found in Leviticus 19:18 containing the command "to love your neighbor as yourself." Also in Galatians 5:14, "For the entire law is fulfilled in keeping this one command: 'Love your neighbor as yourself.'" Jesus, when asked what the greatest commandment is, responded by saying in Matthew 22:37, "'Love the Lord your God with all your heart and with all your soul and with all your mind.' This is the first and greatest commandment. And the second is like it: 'Love your neighbor as yourself.' All the Law and the Prophets hang on these two commandments." This command is "the law" referred to in verse 11.

> "You can either practice being right or practice being kind."
>
> —Anne Lamott, *Plan B: Further Thoughts on Faith*, 99.

James points out that anyone who speaks disdainfully of a sister or brother is, in fact, breaking this royal law (2:8). Continuing in such behavior is no small matter. It does more than break the law; it treats the law as if it did not matter, as if it were not in force. In short, it judges the law and finds it not worthy of adherence.

James knows the central place this command occupied in the ethical teaching of Jesus. What is extremely disturbing to James is that by ignoring this command and in effect, repudiating Christ, these people render the self-description "Christian" a falsehood.

This "speaking ill" of sisters and brothers is closely allied to the ill treatment of sisters and brothers in 2:1-7, and the flagrant refusal to follow the royal law recalls the teaching of James in 2:8-13. The New Testament contains various injunctions against judging (Matthew 7:1-5; Romans 2:1; 1 Corinthians 4:5), but the reason given here, that judging breaks the law, pertains to James alone among the authors of the New Testament.

James 4:12

[12]There is only one Lawgiver and Judge, the one who is able to save and destroy. But you—who are you to judge your neighbor?

As in 2:10-11 James is not content to allow his case to rest on the meager foundation of the law itself. Rather he discusses the law in terms of the personal authority of God who stands behind the law (4:12). Here James is again in touch with a widely held tradition, that Christians should not judge others. Certainly it is a part of the Jesus tradition, for Jesus says in Matthew 7:1, "Do not judge, or you too will be judged" (see also Romans 2:1; 1 Corinthians 4:5).

Only God has the right to judge, as he is the lawgiver (Psalm 9:20). God alone, as Peter Davids points out, has authority over life and death (Genesis 18:25; Deuteronomy 32:39) and only he has the ultimate power to save or to destroy (1Samuel 2:6; Matthew 10:28).

In both Testaments all judgment is assigned to God. Judgment on the part of human beings, therefore, is lodged within the wider context of God's judgment. God assigns to Jesus the task of judging. Jesus is God's representative, though the authority to judge rests with God. The Gospel of John clearly adheres to this pattern. John knows that God is the judge, as in John 8:50 Jesus says, "I am not seeking glory for myself, but there is one who seeks it, and he is the judge." John also argues that Jesus has been delegated the authority to judge by God, for in John 5:22 Jesus says, "The Father judges no one, but has entrusted all judgment to the Son." That Jesus judges in faithfulness to God's appointment is affirmed in John 5:30 when Jesus says, "I judge only as I hear, and my judgment is just." When Jesus says, "Do not judge, or you too will be judged (Matthew 7:1)," he is reflecting the awesome and fearful nature of the task.

To the church God has delegated the task of judging in matters which affect its members. For this reason James and Paul can and do judge. However, they remind us that in judging we are acting in God's stead, and therefore exceptional care and restraint needs to be observed. God does not take it lightly when his name and honor are invoked inappropriately. To render judgment in the flippant, arrogant, and harsh fashion which some in his church have been doing, James finds reprehensible and foolhardy. God will defend the cause of those maligned.

According to James when we judge others we not only misappropriate to ourselves what belongs to God alone (it's like someone asking, "Who made *you* God?"), but we also invite and pronounce judgment upon ourselves. This is not meant to exclude an honest and healthy discussion among believers, but it is to make clear a strong warning that the line which demarks proper from sinful dialogue is easily and often unknowingly crossed. There is a difference in "confronting" others for the purpose of building up and "condemnation" for the purpose of tearing down. James points out that none of us is without stain and we are deserving of the same judgment which we so righteously place at the feet of others. It is possible that a part of the sting here is to avoid giving the church an unsavory reputation within the community at large.

In summary, three points are prominent. 1) God alone has the right to judge. 2) God at times delegates that responsibility. He delegated it to Jesus, and in certain functions he delegates it to us. When exercising this role, however, we serve not as our own agents, but we serve as the representatives of God. 3) We often judge inappropriately. When we use slander we are breaking trust with God, and in so doing we are, in fact, judging ourselves and we place ourselves in jeopardy.

READ BETWEEN THE LINES

- What is "the law" referring to?
- In judging others how do we judge "the law" and the lawgiver?
- Are we never to judge fellow Christians? Explain.

WELCOME TO MY WORLD

- How should I respond to Christians I see acting problematically?
- How will I respond if I hear someone smearing another person in my presence?
- Is there someone I need to apologize to because of the judgmental words that came out of my mouth?
- Do I need to ask God for the grace to change the words that come out of my mouth?

Boasting About Tomorrow

James now addresses (verses 13-17) the unhealthy fascination with the making of money, which James counters with a reminder that money is only temporary. What again binds this passage together and to those before is the power of the tongue, here understood primarily in the individual sense. It is the instrument used to boast of such empty, unimportant things as wealth and status.

James 4:13-14

13Now listen, you who say, "Today or tomorrow we will go to this or that city, spend a year there, carry on business and make money." 14Why, you do not even know what will happen tomorrow. What is your life? You are a mist that appears for a little while and then vanishes.

In verse 13 we have an example of the educated Greek style of James, as it begins with the construction, *"age nun,"* translated by the NIV as "now listen." The construction is rare in the New Testament, being found only here and in 5:1. It is fairly common, however, in the world of Hellenistic literature. The term is meant to convey tones of insistent and even harsh address. While there is some debate as to the identity of the group intended by the phrase "you who say," there is no reason to suppose that James does not have in mind members of the Christian community.

Many argue that the absence of the term "brothers and sisters" indicates that James is now referring to some outside the church, but this is not as strong a position as is often supposed, for James has already referred to members of the church in harsh terms without the designation "brothers and sisters." Also, James 4:15 contains the phrase "if it is the Lord's will," which surely is a marker that Christians are in view. In any event, we have here a group of merchants with some close ties to the church.

Verse 13 also contains a quotation; presumably James has heard that such statements have been on the lips of the merchants in the city. There is a strong Old Testament tradition of distrust of merchants and traders (Proverbs 20:23; Micah 6:11), but this does not seem to be the appropriate background here.

There also seems to be a desire to make a profit as the towering priority that has overshadowed everything else. If this is correct, it recalls the merchants who, in the words of Amos, trample the needy as they anxiously await the end of the Sabbath so they can make more money (Amos 8:4-5). The parable of the rich fool who relies on his stored wealth also comes to mind (Luke 12:16-21).

James is not arguing against the making of money, or even against the desire to make money, as he is against the attitude of self-contained certainty, the same smug attitude that marked the teaching of the false teachers that leaves no room for God. Such certainty exposes an attitude that does not take God seriously enough, a state of mind for which the making of money outstrips devotion to God in importance. The desire betrays friendship with the world, and therefore hostility with God.

Beyond this, of course, is another sin, for they have not seen the poor as their sisters and brothers. They have not shared with them, but have showed favoritism. There is no discernible difference in their lives for having come to know Jesus.

At this point it is proper to ask about these traders and merchants. Sophie Laws insightfully argues that these must be traders on an international scale, as the verb used by James (*emporeusometha*) indicates a distinction between the wholesale traveling traders (*emporoi*) and the local merchants (*kapeloi*). More significant is the allusion to traveling to other cities.

As Gerd Theissen has noted, travel was expensive. Of course travel does not necessarily indicate the wealth of the traveler. But someone with wealth paid the bill. Yet we know of many New Testament Christians with that kind of wealth. Chloe, a female leader in the church in Corinth, had enough money to send some of her "people" with a message to Paul (1 Corinthians 1:11). So the reference to travel and the considerable resources such travel indicates does not necessarily preclude these traders from membership in the church.

In verse 14 in spite of all their careful planning (all the verbs in the quotation in 4:13 are in the future tense: "will go," "will spend," "will carry," "will make") the future is uncertain. There is a clear connection to the rich in 1:10-11 who, in spite of their feelings of security, will be brought low. There James said that the rich and their riches will fade like a flower. This is a reminder of the transitory nature of riches and human life. Here the life of human beings can be compared to a mist that vanishes even as it is apprehended, with an ease and swiftness that takes the breath away.

The American social and cultural landscape is studded with success stories like that of billionaires Bill Gates, Warren Buffet, Michael Bloomberg, Jeff Bezos, and Mark Zuckerberg. It may even still be possible to become a millionaire buying real estate with no money down, but as James reminds us, this is not the point. There is a transitory nature of financial wealth. Financial affluence is like the mist, it can disappear even as we grasp it because not only is wealth difficult to accumulate, but it is often difficult to maintain.

Of course, for most Americans financial affluence is beyond the realm of possibility. The AFL-CIO notes that in 1965 on average a CEO made 44 times the salary of the average worker. In 2012 the difference was 380 times. As we write this the United States is in the deepest, longest recession since the Great Depression of the 1930s.

Old Testament parallels are instructive. Proverbs 27:1 says, "Do not boast about tomorrow, for you do not know what a day may bring," and Hosea 13:3 in speaking of the people who have turned from God says, "Therefore they will be like the morning mist, like the early dew that disappears, like chaff swirling from a threshing floor, like smoke escaping through a window."

These are the same images as in James: Making plans without considering God is evidence of absurdity. Life is transitory. The parable of Jesus concerning the house built upon sand comes quickly to mind (Matthew 7:24-27). We rely on a myriad of resources which are, in the words of the Bible, only mist. Life is unpredictable, James says, and we are foolish if we rely on anything other than God.

For James the real question is how to approach life when the outcome is uncertain. His answer is to trust in God's graciousness, not human plans. This is, in fact, one of the central messages of the Prophets. To trust in one's own devices is foolish in light of the fact that one can trust in God. There is a simple beauty to this truth, but we struggle with it every day. Even those who have learned it the hard way fall back into old patterns of calling out to God only in dire circumstances. God desires for us to develop daily patterns of trust in and friendship with him.

James 4:15-17

15Instead, you ought to say, "If it is the Lord's will, we will live and do this or that." 16As it is, you boast in your arrogant schemes. All such boasting is evil. 17If anyone, then, knows the good they ought to do and doesn't do it, it is sin for them.

In verse 15, James is not against planning or setting a

schedule. The first step in good planning is to ask God what should be done first. We can plan ahead but we must hold those plans loosely and be open to God rearranging those plans. It's about seeking God's will in every matter of our lives. It is not merely saying a flippant "God willing" and then doing our own thing. James wants such planning to be given its proper priority and none higher. Proverbs 19:21 says, "Many are the plans in a person's heart, but it is the Lord's purpose that prevails." Many people say they believe in God but in reality they are practical atheists. They make decisions and plans for the future as if God didn't exist.

> How foolish it is for people to ignore the will of God. It is like going through the dark jungles without a map, or over the stormy seas without a compass. When we visited Mammoth Cave in Kentucky, I was impressed with the maze of tunnels and the dense darkness when the lights were turned off. When we got to the "Pulpit Rock," the man in charge of the tour gave a five-word sermon from it: "Stay close to your guide." Good counsel indeed!
>
> —Warren W. Wiersbe, *Be Mature, James*, 140.

"'My food,'" said Jesus, "is to do the will of him who sent me and to finish his work" (John 4:34). Paul also in his letters referred to the will of God as he shared his plans with his friends (Romans 1:10; 15:32; 1 Corinthians 4:19; 16:7). Paul did not consider the will of God a chain that shackled him; rather, it was a key that opened doors and set him free.

> I find that many youth workers tend to be creative but disorganized. I teach my students in one section of a youth ministry class the value of planning ahead and time management. I talk about how the puritans loved the Latin phrase "*Deo Volente*"

meaning "God willing" or "If the Lord wills." They filled their speech and correspondence with that phrase. Years ago Methodists regularly signed their letters with the shortened Latin abbreviation "DV." In every aspect of our life we need to ask, is this the Lord's will and to be open to change when necessary.

—Les

In Verse 16 the merchants are not rebuked for the wealth they possess, or even for the pursuit of more. Rather, the rub is that they do so without reference to God, and they boast about it. As Sophie Laws observes, the primary issue is spiritual, not material or even (primarily) social. Boasting in our own accomplishments and/or in our own plans, on our own terms, is the issue. As long as God is not in control of such endeavors, boasting is evil.

Two points need to be made. 1) The saying of Jesus regarding almsgiving ("So when you give to the needy, do not announce it with trumpets, as the hypocrites do in the synagogues and on the streets, to be honored by others. Truly I tell you, they have received their reward in full."— Matthew 6:2) illuminates this passage. The attitude God desires seeks his favor, not the praise of the world. 2) "Evil" is a strong word. Other less harsh words were at the command of James, yet he chose this one. Boasting is not for James a trivial matter. This boasting is the sin mentioned in 4:13.

The merchants plan and carry on as if God were unimportant or did not even exist. Instead, they should have made their plans in prayer, and in the expectation that God may in fact change these plans. The merchants may be superficially pious in church, but their attitude if not their actions are boastful of their independence from God.

In verse 17, James shifts to the third person singular

from the second person plural, indicating that he is quoting a proverb (as in 2:13; 3:18). Sophie Laws wonders how this verse connects with the others in this passage, but then she believes that the merchants are not members of the church. If however, the merchants are members of the church the connection is obvious, and James is saying, "Now that you know what is right, do it!" James is possibly commenting here on Proverbs 3:27-28, "Do not withhold good from those to whom it is due, when it is in your power to act. Do not say to your neighbor, 'Come back tomorrow and I'll give it to you'—when you already have it with you."

There are similar sayings in a variety of sources from the ancient world. Ultimately, the precise identification of the source is not of critical importance. James here argues that sins of both "commission" and "omission" are grievous, especially when done knowingly. The making of plans as though the future is certain is itself a sin, because functionally it is a denial of God, either his importance or even his very existence. Then to boast about it is a further sin. James may perhaps be building on the saying of Jesus in Luke 12:47: "The servant who knows the master's will and does not get ready or does not do what the master wants will be beaten with many blows." Knowledge of "the master's will" places him under a moral obligation to do "the master's will."

READ BETWEEN THE LINES

- Is James against planning ahead? Explain.
- How do both the poor and the rich seek security in money?
- How is life, wealth, health, and job security like a mist?
- What is the difference between verses 13 and 15?
- Are we to simply say, "God willing" and then go on with our plans? Explain.
- How does James explain sin in verse 16?

WELCOME TO MY WORLD

- Would I describe wealthy people as self-confident or humble?
- When does my planning turn into boasting?
- How do I feel knowing my life is but a mist?
- How will I combine my appointment calendar with God's will?
- How will I now make plans for the future after reading verses 13-15?
- How does God want me to view the future?
- How detailed is the will of God for my life?
- If I knew I had a month to live what would I do?

Warning to Rich Oppressors

James 5:1

¹Now listen, you rich people, weep and wail because of the misery that is coming on you.

Verse 1 stands as a sharp introductory warning. It is intended to warn the rich of their coming destruction, and although there is no clear call to repentance here, it is not unreasonable to surmise that such is the implication.

As in 4:13, James begins this section with the rare (in the New Testament) phrase *age nun* ("Now listen"). Today we would say "Look here!" or "Listen up!" This group (landowners) is not the same as the "you who say" of 4:13 (the merchants). However, to the common people the two groups are essentially alike, in that both have money. These two distinct groups have essentially one malady: an irrational desire for and trust in wealth. James calls for a sudden opening of the eyes, for the rich to see that they are, in fact, oppressing the poor. This is directed to those unrighteous rich people who claim to be followers of Christ. In a roundabout way James is also telling the poor Christians not to envy the rich, ungodly or otherwise.

These wealthy people must "weep and wail." "Weep" (*klaio*) means to respond to disaster in a rightful manner. The proper response to disaster is to weep from the depths of one's being in grief and remorse. "Wail" (*ololuzo*) means to howl, especially as a result of sudden and unexpected evil or regret. There is no shortage of Old Testament parallels to this idea (Lamentations 1:1-2; Isaiah 13:6; 15:2-3, 5; Jeremiah 13:7).

This remorse is justified because the lot of these rich is misery (*talaiporias*, a word used only here and in Romans 3:16 in the New Testament). The reason is not their wealth *per se*, but the fact that they have not sought to use their wealth to alleviate the sufferings of the poor.

James 5:2-3

2Your wealth has rotted, and moths have eaten your clothes. 3Your gold and silver are corroded. Their corrosion will testify against you and eat your flesh like fire. You have hoarded wealth in the last days.

Having condemned the wealthy landowners for their indifference, James now points out that riches are worthless when it comes to eternal salvation. The terms used here ("wealth," "clothes," "gold and silver") comprise a standard catalogue of riches in the ancient world, especially if "wealth" refers to land and its produce. The produce of the land has "rotted" and the clothing has been eaten by moths (Job 13:28). The gold and silver have corroded or rusted. Technically these metals do not rust, but James is writing with the eye of a prophet. James is characterizing wealth as transitory (it comes and goes) and in the process of decay.

James employs these three verbs in the perfect tense. The decay has not taken place, and yet with the eye of a prophet the result is as clear to James as the daybreak is to the watchers on the wall (Isaiah 62:6). The wealthy still enjoy the benefit of their wealth and station, but unless they repent, their destiny is set, and James can see it.

In Matthew 6:20 Jesus said, "But store up for yourself treasures in heaven, where moths and vermin do not destroy." This corrosion acts not only on the metals, but with far more serious import upon the flesh of the wealthy just as a fire ravages all before it. The idea, of course, is that their wealth will accuse these landowners, especially since in spite of the signs, they have continued to hoard wealth even though it is the last days (v. 3).

This is not to say that James is imagining an imminent *parousia* (i.e., second coming, last days). Rather the thought is that just as it would be criminally ridiculous to hoard wealth when the *parousia* is imminent, so Christians who have heard the message of Jesus and yet shortchange their workers and hoard wealth while their Christian brothers and sisters are needy of even the basic necessities are morally liable. In spite of their planning, the treasure that awaits them is not their fine clothing or their gold, but rather misery.

Like the citizens of Carthage who partied while their city was under siege and then stormed by King Genseric in AD 439, the wealthy landowners have been about a task which seemed important to them at the time, but which upon further reflection could only be judged idiotic. Of course the idea could also be taken figuratively, that they have stored up a "treasure" of punishment soon to be delivered. James' warning is not against saving money. James is against selfish hoarding that not only affects the person but everyone else in that person's life.

> He is no fool who gives what he cannot keep to gain that which he cannot lose.
> —Jim Elliot

James provides four reasons for the wealthy landowners to weep. Their wealth is temporal, and subject to the ravages of time; they are guilty of a crime against their sisters and brothers; they will be judged and condemned for this selfish use of temporal goods; and they have been adding to their material treasure as if the world would go on forever.

Hetty Green was once the richest woman in America. At her death she was worth up to $100 million. There are many tales (of various degrees of accuracy) regarding her stinginess. When she heard that her aunt Sylvia had willed most of her $2 million to charity, she challenged the will's validity in court but lost the case.

Her frugality extended to family life. Her son Ned broke his leg as a child, and Hetty tried to have him admitted in a free clinic for the poor. When she was recognized, she stormed away vowing to treat the wounds herself. After procrastinating about seeking treatment for the boy she finally brought her son to other doctors (while also trying home remedies).Her son's leg was amputated after years of unsuccessful treatment.

And when she was on her deathbed at eighty-one, her nurses were not permitted to wear uniforms, for old Hetty would never have died in peace if she suspected that she was paying expensive registered nurses' wages. Money was her master. She lived for it, worshiped it.

James 5:4-5

⁴Look! The wages you failed to pay the workers who mowed your fields are crying out against you. The cries of the harvesters have reached the ears of the Lord Almighty. ⁵You have lived on earth in luxury and self-indulgence. You have fattened yourselves in the day of slaughter.

James now lists specific behaviors that contributed to the hoarding of wealth. For one thing, they have not paid their hired laborers their due. These workers may have hired themselves out to the wealthy landowners. The workers and harvesters would live day to day on the money they earned, often on the verge of starvation. If workers did not receive their daily pay their family would not eat. The wages which were due to the workers are now in the treasury of the landowner.

These very wages cry out to the iniquity of injustice, just as the blood of Abel cried out from the ground concerning the sin of Cain (Genesis 4:10). This is far more serious than the landowners have imagined. Moreover, the Bible makes it clear that God is the defender of the poor and oppressed.

Because God has already heard the cry, the voice of judgment against the wealthy has already begun to sound. James says that the double cry (of the workers and of the wages) has reached the ears of "the Lord Almighty." Here the NIV has done a disservice, for James uses the expression *kurios sabaoth*, which may be better translated, "the Lord of Hosts" or "Lord of the armies" (a phrase appearing only here and in Romans 9:29 in the New Testament). The phrase conjures up the image of God going to war against the wealthy to defend his oppressed poor.

In verse 5 James turns his attention from the hardship imposed on others to the ease and slothfulness of the wealthy. He says they have lived lives of "luxury" and gross "self-indulgence." They are living an exorbitant lifestyle. The strength of the terms suggests that there is more here than simply a life of pleasure. The terms imply such superabundance that this life of luxury is pursued at the expense of others, and with an attitude of unfeeling dismissal toward them.

The phrase "on earth" (literally "on the land") rightly identifies land ownership and agriculture as the basis of real and inherited wealth in antiquity. For example, Pliny (*Epistulae*, 3.19) says there are three ways to make money: inheritance, loaning money with interest, and marrying into money. By inheritance he meant land, which was the only sure basis for wealth. The opening phrase, "you have lived" also points with accuracy to the fact that wealth tended to be hereditary. Almost nobody in this time period was able to pull themselves up by their own bootstraps.

The point of verse 5 recalls the parable of the rich man and Lazarus in Luke 16:19–31. Here as well as there the rich have received in this life all the comfort they will have. They can expect nothing but torment in the next life.

Martin wisely points out that unlike the merchants in 4:13-17 who do wrong, these landowners fail to do anything, even in the face of great misery! This is supported by the term "lives for pleasure" (1 Timothy 5:6), a word James uses to point to a great sin, a denial of God and of our common humanity.

This point he makes with astonishing clarity in the final sentence of verse 5: "You have fattened yourselves in the day of slaughter." Few behaviors are more despicable than to profit from the deaths of others. The NIV does not do justice to the force of the Greek text. Swindoll writes, "Like a pig fattened for slaughter, these wealthy don't even know that as they selfishly gorge on the pleasures of life, they are eating and drinking judgment upon themselves." This conveys the sense of complete self-interest and indulging all lusts without thought of shame.

"In the day of slaughter" is a somewhat problematic phrase. The verse clearly betrays an eschatological dimension, yet the preposition *en* is used, not *eis*, which one would expect if a future orientation were in view. Perhaps the best way to resolve the problem is to understand that for James the day of reckoning has already begun—the day of judgment as well as the day of the slaughter of the enemies of God (Jeremiah 46:10). This would harmonize nicely with the Gospel accounts of the sayings of Jesus, as we have seen.

James 5:6

⁶You have condemned and murdered the innocent one, who was not opposing you.

The final accusation aimed at the landed class is their plotting of the wrongful treatment and even murder of the innocent (v. 6). This verse presents difficulty if taken literally, but apart from the disgust such a reading creates, there are little if any grounds, grammatical or otherwise, from seeing this verse in any way other than literal. This death referred to here may be the result of starvation caused by the withholding of wages.

Or perhaps like the powerful landed gentry everywhere in the empire, these men saw themselves as the kings of their own land (Amos 5:11-12). Many controlled the courts. Their victims do not oppose them, probably, because they could not.

Plutarch (Greek historian, biographer) tells us that Cato (Roman statesman) considered himself the law on his estates, presiding over even capital trials. The other practices endorsed by Cato, such as the chain-gang for slaves and his advice that the owner or the representative of the owner claim to themselves the role of judge and jury, demonstrates with crystal clarity that Roman justice was only for Roman citizens.

Some have suggested an ancient tradition that suggests that the "innocent" (literally, "righteous") one is Jesus himself (Acts 3:14; 7:53; 1 Peter 3:18; 1 John 2:1). The wealthy should understand that God takes it personally when we treat others like garbage, deserving not even our attention as they die. In Matthew 25:31-46 Jesus says that he considers our treatment of the poor and the imprisoned and the thirsty to be our treatment of him.

Today's farmer uses complex and expensive machinery. But in the ancient world there were no such options. Instead, wealthy landowners who fancied themselves "farmers" employed slaves and poor free persons on their land. These farmers were among the wealthiest in the empire. Today the super-rich rarely make their money in agricultural production.

James calls us to open our eyes, to see that as evangelicals in the wealthiest nation in human history, we bear a responsibility for understanding the power and peril of our wealth, and to use it responsibly. Like the Romans, we esteem people for their wealth, and not so often for their soul. Popular magazines glamorize high society and wealth, whether the source of this wealth is business, entertainment, or sports.

> I used to think when I was a child, that Christ might have been exaggerating when he warned about the dangers of wealth. Today I know better. I know how hard it is to be rich and still keep the milk of human kindness. Money has a dangerous way of putting scales on one's eyes, a dangerous way of freezing people's hands, eyes, lips and hearts.
>
> —Dom Heldert Camara, *Revolution Through Peace*, Harper, New York, 1971, 142-143, quoted in Ronald J. Sider, *Rich Christians in an Age of Hunger: A Biblical Study*, Paulist Press, New York, 1977, 122.

James pronounces a stern warning to the wealthy today. James condemns an attitude toward wealth which deadens the wealthy toward others and causes them to live in excess even as their brothers and sisters are in need. Human law does not require charity or genuine concern for our neighbors. But God's law and character demands a higher order of living from us.

James does not condemn riches *per se*. The Bible does condemn acquiring wealth by illegal means or for illegal purposes, and the wealthy who have not sought to use their wealth to alleviate the sufferings of the poor. The Old Testament prophets Amos, Isaiah, and Jeremiah all exposed the selfishness of the rich who robbed the poor. James is upset with people who worship money more than God; when material things come between you and God, then your whole sense of values becomes irrational. Money has an attractive power that can be lethal in its effects if not kept in check. The *love of money* is a root of all kinds of evil (1 Timothy 6:10).

American evangelicals are among the wealthiest persons alive, possessing money and influence. So the appeal of James resounds across the centuries to our ears. We must open our eyes to the Scriptures and our ears to God, and prayerfully consider how best to use our money. Our failure to act, says James, is a sin more grievous than we have imagined.

READ BETWEEN THE LINES

- Who is James addressing whom he calls "rich people"?
- What is the difference between the "merchant" and the "landowning" people?
- Why is James so critical of wealthy people?
- Is James against the rich and making money? Explain.
- What is the difference between 'hoarding" and "prudent savings"?
- What are the consequences of misusing riches?
- What are the wealthy to do with their wealth?
- What is the "last days"?
- How do the fields cry out against the wealthy?
- How is the life of self-absorbed, irresponsible luxury equal to murder?
- Who is the "innocent one"?
- How is this passage similar and different from James 4:13–17?

WELCOME TO MY WORLD

- What advice would I give Bill Gates (Microsoft), Warren Buffet (investments), the Waltons (Walmart), Jeff Bezos (Amazon), and Mark Zuckerberg (Facebook)?
- Do I think of myself as rich? Explain.
- How has wealth tainted me?
- Is my bank account my security? Explain.
- What should be the basis of my security?

- Does my church go after the rich people in our community? Explain.
- How can I use my resources to help the poor and needy?
- How have some of the rich today oppressed others (the needy, poor) for personal gain?

Patience in Suffering

James 5:7-11 is a call to patient living under adverse circumstances. The root word for patience, *makrothymeo*, occurs four times in these five verses. Another term, *hypomone*, which the NIV renders as "perseverance" occurs twice. The two words are close parallels, and in Colossians 1:11 are virtual synonyms. The root *makrothymeo* carries with it the idea of waiting with calm and expectancy, and the words associated with *hypomone* tend to convey the sense of patient endurance and fortitude.

The passage consists of one tight argument, but with three discernible components. In the first (verses 7-8) James calls us to patience and then provides an example from everyday life. He draws the conclusion that we too should be patient. Next (verse 9) James affirms that patience must be mixed with the harmony that results from controlled speech and behavior; thus he counsels against complaining about one another. In the final section (verses 10-11) he returns to the issue of patience, citing the biblical examples of the prophets and Job.

There is much that binds this section with the one just previous, especially the return of the term "brothers and sisters," which James here as elsewhere uses to remind his readers that although he has offered them strong rebuke, he is their brother and they are all one in Christ. James shifts audiences in this next section of Scripture, while in 5:1-6 the emphasis is on the wealthy, here the lion's share of James' thought is directed to the poor answering the question, "How do we respond rightly when we are wronged?"

James 5:7

7Be patient, then, brothers and sisters, until the Lord's coming. See how the farmer waits for the land to yield its valuable crop, patiently waiting for the autumn and spring rains.

Verse 7 offers up an interesting bit of Christology. Christians are instructed to be patient until the Lord's coming (*parousia tou kuriou;* literally, "coming of the Lord"). In verses 10 and 11 James uses the word *kurios* in reference to God in the Old Testament examples of Job and the prophets. It is difficult to see how this present phrase in verse 7 can be applied to anyone other than Jesus Christ. Jesus Christ, in other words, is Lord.

While we are on ground too weak to build a grand Christological edifice, the implication should not be missed. Many argue that James is wholly without Christology. While it is an accurate assessment that Christological concerns and language are largely absent from James, here a statement of high Christology is present. This *parousia* will include Jesus Christ setting the oppressed free (Luke 4:16-21). But the waiting is a long process, and the temptation to criticize will be overpowering. For this reason James offers for consideration a series of illustrations.

As a practical illustration of such patience, James refers to a farmer who waits patiently for harvest time, and for the late autumn and early spring rains. In the eastern Mediterranean two seasons of rain are both normal and necessary for a successful crop. The emphasis here is double, not only upon patience, but also upon the surety of the farmer that the rains and the harvest will indeed come, each in its due season. This waiting is hard psychologically, for before the whims of weather which determine the success of the crop the farmer is helpless. As N.T. Wright has pointed out, "Farmers learn to live with the rhythm of the seasons. Our frantic modern society, which wants to have every vegetable in the shops all year round and so brings them in by plane from far away, has done its best to obliterate the need for patience."

In a similar manner to the farmer the Christian and the Christian community must wait patiently for the coming of the Lord, for there is nothing to be done to speed the *parousia* on its way. The waiting is often hard. Difficulties within the community must be dealt with, and the correct understanding and practice of the faith and works dynamic must be taught and maintained. It is easily misunderstood, as the letter itself demonstrates. This is not a passive resignation, but rather patient expectation waiting on the Lord.

> I spent a part of my childhood on my uncle's grain farm in the Sacramento Valley of California. Each October my uncle planted wheat and oats, and through the long winter he watched as the plants sprouted, and then grew strong and tall. Finally, in the heat of June, he began harvest. The end result is the harvest, but the harvest is not possible without the growth accomplished during the long, hard months of winter. So it is with the spiritual life. Our destiny is to be with Christ, but it is often in the crucible of difficulty that God prepares us for that day. James uses the example of the prophets and of Job, persons whose lives were marked by difficult circumstances they often did not understand, but in which God forged their spiritual character. James, as my wife says, desires us to shift our attention from what is happening to us to what God is forming in us.
>
> **—David**

James 5:8

⁸You too, be patient and stand firm, because the Lord's coming is near.

Verse 8 "is near" recalls the Markan account of the opening of Jesus' ministry, as both make use of the same verb, *engizo*. The perfect tense of this verb, *engiken*, is ambiguous, in part because the language of nearness involves ambiguity. When Judas "drew near" to kiss Jesus he made contact with Jesus. So *engiken* can mean "is coming shortly" (as it does here), or it can mean "has arrived." This ambiguity is intentional in Mark 1:15 where Jesus announces, "The time has come....The kingdom of God has come near." Of course *parousia* in James 5:7 is a technical term indicating the coming of Christ.

The preponderance of scholars today interpret this passage to mean James was not expecting an immediate return of Jesus. They support this by pointing out the heavy emphasis of James on being patient and persevering, which he would not do if Christ's return was just a few weeks away. Also James would be aware of Jesus' statement in Matthew 24:36 that no one knows the day or the hour. Although the evidence is mounting that the early church did not anticipate the imminent return of Christ, it must be admitted that this conclusion cannot be dismissed so quickly.

Whether or not James envisioned an imminent return of Christ, perhaps the point here is that as Christians we are to live in community one with another as if the new day has already dawned. This idea reminds his readers that every day ought to be lived with the same devotion to Christian principles and morals as if it were the last day. Otherwise, we will be guilty of apathy "on the day of slaughter" (James 5:5).

The thought of a Christian community has permeated this entire commentary. The word has been used 70 times in this book. This community is not only with God but with each other. Abraham Joshua Heschel said, "When I was young, I admired clever people. Now that I am old, I admire kind people."

I was sitting on a beach one summer day, watching two children, a boy and a girl, playing in the sand. They were hard at work building an elaborate sand castle by the water's edge, with gates and towers and moats and internal passages.

Just when they had nearly finished their project, a big wave came along and knocked it down, reducing it to a heap of wet sand. I expected the children to burst into tears, devastated by what had happened to all their hard work. But they surprised me. Instead, they ran up the shore away from the water, laughing and holding hands, and sat down to build another castle.

I realized that they had taught me an important lesson. All the things in our lives, all the complicated structures we spend so much time and energy creating, are built on sand. Only our relationships to other people endure. Sooner or later, the wave will come along and knock down what we have worked so hard to build up. When that happens, only the person who has somebody's hand to hold will be able to laugh.

—**Rabbi Harold Kushner,** *When All You've Wanted Isn't Enough,* 165-166.

James 5:9

⁹**Don't grumble against one another, brothers and sisters, or you will be judged. The Judge is standing at the door!**

If we are correct in seeing that this passage has as its primary audience the poor who suffer the darts and lethal indifference of the merchants (4:13-17) and the landed gentry (5:1-6), then James in verse 9 has a warning for them as well: In spite of your poor treatment, do not grumble. "Grumble" is a harsh, mean word. We speak of "carrying a grudge." But we don't carry it, we sort of wallow in it. Grudges must be nourished if they are to stay alive. If you give your hurts and injustices to God, they'll diminish in size. God will give you the proper perspective.

The key term here, as Peter Davids notes, is *kat allelon* ("against one another"). James reminds the poor that the wealthy, so often the self-imposed enemies of the poor, are sisters and brothers, fellow believers in Christ. Even understandable feelings of antagonism for what they have suffered at the hands of the indifferent wealthy lays the poor open to judgment. Only Christ, the Judge, has the right to criticize. Internal bickering is an evil that easily can beset and occupy the church, thereby preventing it from its primary task.

Life does bring trials, but no one is served by the cultivation of a spirit of complaining. James would have us remember 3:16 and 4:2: that complaining leads not to peace but to disorder, nor does it do anything to alleviate the real problem. James buttresses his point by reminding his readers that judgment is coming and that he has already enjoined them in the name of the Judge from speaking any kind of evil one against another (4:11). James's image here is similar to John's image in Revelation 3:20, "Here I am! I stand at the door and knock."

James 5:10-11

[10]Brothers and sisters, as an example of patience in the face of suffering, take the prophets who spoke in the name of the Lord. [11]As you know, we count as blessed those who have persevered. You have heard of Job's perseverance and have seen what the Lord finally brought about. The Lord is full of compassion and mercy.

James clearly expects his readers to be familiar with these examples in James 5:10-11. It also confirms our earlier decision to see the landowners of 5:1-6 as members of the Christian community, and familiar enough with the Old Testament to see in their own behavior a parallel to the wealthy castigated by the prophets.

The prophets as the messengers of God experienced suffering (for example: Jeremiah, Ezekiel, Daniel). But the prophets endured, patiently and hopefully, waiting for the judgment and the mercy of God. Sophie Laws notes the growing tradition of the prophets as martyrs, but also comments that only Zechariah (2 Chronicles 24:20-22) met a violent death. Of course one can be a martyr without suffering persecution by death. The prophets "spoke in the name of the Lord," and this indicates that in this world those who assume the name of God as their banner will suffer.

Such a course of action also brings with it the high honor and regard of earning the label "blessed" (verse 11). The grammar of this verse suggests that "blessedness" is reserved for those who have been found faithful to the end, while one like Job enjoyed its experience while still alive. The Greek verb *makarizo* can also be used to mean "fortunate" or "happy," although neither word carries the same spiritual weight of the English word "blessed" (see 1:12). But perhaps primary in James' mind is that those who have gone into the presence of God with such a life of perseverance are truly "blessed." This idea that blessedness is a reward for those who endure is widely represented in the New Testament and is found on the lips of Jesus (Matthew 5:10-12; 23:29-36).

From the example of the prophets James turns to the specific example of Job. Job was a wealthy man. Then he lost everything (his wealth, family—except for his wife and she told him to commit suicide—and his health). It is difficult to find a greater example of suffering than Job. However, this choice by James of Job seems odd to many interpreters, for Job complained bitterly to God. They suggest that James may have been thinking of the apocryphal *Testament of Job* in which Job is patient while his wife does the complaining. There is much that commends this hypothesis.

While this line of thinking is attractive, perhaps it accepts a too simple reading of Job. In fact, Job remains faithful to the picture of God which he possessed, and questioned only the accuracy of that picture. Like that of the Psalmist (Psalm 69:1) Job's complaint to God was a complaint born out of faith.

This is encouraging. God understands our tears. He knows we are clay. He accepts our questions. God requires that we recognize there are processes at work beyond our comprehension. A plan far bigger than us is moving toward completion.

> Job's is no groveling, passive, unquestioning submission; Job struggled and questioned and sometimes even defied, but the flame of faith was never extinguished in his heart.
> —William Barclay

Job endured incomprehensible personal, financial, and physical loss, yet he refused to give in to the revenge reflex. As a result of his sufferings he gained greater knowledge of God, which may indeed be the purpose of God and the hope James has as the result of the sufferings that are the background to this passage. In the same way, those who patiently endure hardship today can rely on God's promise of ultimate reward and blessing, whether in this life or in the life to come.

James employs a phrase which has occasioned much speculation: The phrase the NIV renders "have seen what the Lord finally brought about." The Greek term *to telos* (finally) has other possible translations and can render the sentence to be a reference to either Jesus' death or to his *parousia* (the anticipated return of Jesus Christ to the earth). However, it is more likely that *to telos* refers to the "purpose" or "plan" of the Lord. The plan of the Lord in the life of the believer, as James has been at great pains to point out, is to live a life of Christian virtue based upon accurate teaching. The successful pursuit of such a course of action will lead to being called "blessed."

> Julie Lindsey was working the late shift at a hotel just south of Montgomery, Alabama. Her part-time employment helped pay her college bills as she finished school. She was a devout

believer. But her belief was tested the night two men held a gun to her head and forced her into their truck. She was robbed, repeatedly raped and left handcuffed to a tree. It was two o'clock in the morning before she was rescued.

The nightmare nearly destroyed her. She couldn't function, the hotel fired her, and she dropped out of school. In her words, she was "shattered, lost, and bewildered." ...

How does such a tragedy have a place in God's plan? In time, Julie learned the answer to that question. Listen to her words:

After this experience, I spent a great deal of time thinking about God...I searched and I prayed for understanding. I longed to be healed...My spirit and faith were sorely tested; my spiritual journey in the months that followed was painful, but also wonderful. God allowed me to profit from an awful and devastating event. So many good things are in my life now. I have wonderful friends—most of whom I would never have met or known were it not for this experience. I have a job that allows me to work with and serve crime victims. I have a deeper relationship with God. I am spiritually wiser and more mature. I have been blessed beyond what I can tell in these pages, and I am very grateful. Romans 8:28 came alive in my life: "All things work together for good for those who love God and are called according to his purpose."

Now I ask you, who won? Julie now has a ministry speaking to groups about God's mercy and healing. Can't you imagine the devil groaning with each message? What he intended for evil, God used for good. Satan unknowingly advanced the cause of the kingdom. Rather than destroy a disciple, he strengthened a disciple.

Think about that the next time evil flaunts its cape and races across your stage. Remember, the final act has already been scripted. And the day Christ comes will be the end of evil.

—Max Lucado, *Life Lessons, James*, 106.

God does not enjoy watching his people suffer. He allows them to face such pain because a greater good is produced. Suffering is used by God to produce Christians who are mature, who understand the dynamic of faith and deeds, and who are about the task of peace and not disorder.

> In an age of instant solutions and results, the word *finally* grinds against our will. We would much rather read "quickly" or "immediately" than be reminded again that God's timing and priorities are different from ours.
> —*Life Application Bible Commentary*, 132.

Catherine of Genoa encourages us to throw ourselves into the arms of God, and to rely not on worldly possessions. Her biography bears out the truth of her words. Catherine was born into a prosperous and important religious family in 1447. In 1463 she married a man committed to wealth and its increase, and this was the source of no little tension. But when her husband lost the bulk of his fortune the two of them decided to live and work among the poor in Genoa. In this life she found greater joy and fulfillment than when she enjoyed wealth and ease. Catherine teaches us that the world and material goods cannot compare with joy that comes with spiritual growth.

Thomas à Kempis became a monk at the age of nineteen in 1399. The great spiritual treatise, *The Imitation of Christ*, is his most significant work (though some believe that it was written by Gerhard Groote and edited by Thomas). In the following passage Thomas discusses the usefulness of difficulties:

> And yet, temptations can be useful to us even though they seem to cause us nothing but pain. They are useful because they

> can make us humble, they can cleanse us, and they can teach us. All of the saints passed through times of temptation and tribulation, and they used them to make progress in the spiritual life...No one is completely free of temptations because the source of temptation is in ourselves...We cannot win this battle by running away alone; the key to victory is true humility and patience; in them we overcome the enemy.
>
> —Thomas à Kempis, *The Imitation of Christ*, 13.2-3.

The purpose and plan of God includes his "compassion and mercy." We have seen these themes before (4:6), but James knows that human beings are not only in constant need of the assurance of grace and forgiveness, but in constant need of the fact of grace and forgiveness as well. God is good.

READ BETWEEN THE LINES

- What is the "Lord's coming" referring to?
- How is being patient for the Lord's coming similar to a farmer waiting for the land to yield a valuable crop?
- What does it mean to "stand firm"?
- Why are the people in the church grumbling against one another?
- How is Job an example of patience during suffering?
- What is the value in suffering?
- Why is James telling the poor not to sink to the level of those who have wronged them?

WELCOME TO MY WORLD

- In the midst of suffering and difficulty have I doubted God's presence and faithfulness? Explain.
- What will I need to be able to stand firm?

- How difficult is it for me not to complain when faced with challenging times?
- Who is a living example to me of patience and perseverance?
- How have I shown impatience by grumbling?
- How can I develop a grateful attitude?
- What encouragement do I get from Job's story?
- Who are some friends God has brought into my life to help me get through tough times?

Do Not Swear

James is about to conclude his letter. He does so by focusing on three themes which dominated the beginning of his letter: speech, prayer, and suffering. Just as the letter began with a double opening, James presents us with something of a double ending. In 5:1-7 he discussed trials, rich vs. poor and pure speech, three themes which dominate the letter as a whole. Here he places a cap on his discussion by emphasizing pure speech (prayer) and its power in times of adversity.

Verses 12-18 have two natural sections. Verse 12 is an injunction against the making of oaths, while verses 13-18 concern prayer. The passage moves from the situation of one who is suffering, to one who is joyful, back to one who is suffering. What binds the entire passage together is that both sections have to do with how we address God, and with the use of the tongue.

James 5:12

¹²Above all, my brothers and sisters, do not swear—not by heaven or by earth or by anything else. All you need to say is a simple "Yes" or "No." Otherwise you will be condemned.

"Above all" (*pro panton*) means "most importantly" or "but especially." However, given the care with which James has developed other themes, especially, for example, the great stress he has placed on patience, it would be odd indeed if James were to say that his message concerning oaths he regards as the single most important one in the entire letter. Rather, the term ought to be understood as "finally," or "to sum up." James is alerting his readers that the letter is about to conclude.

Any attempt to defend the present placement of this saying must show how it connects either with what has gone before or what is to come. As many have noted, this saying appears out of place. However, when seen as an inappropri-ate use of the tongue in contradistinction to the proper uses pointed out in 5:13-18, it is clear that this verse has a right-ful place here. This, of course, connects the verse with what comes after. But what about the preceding section? Ralph Martin believes that Reicke is correct when he argues that the swearing of oaths is a sign of the impatience displayed by the poor who live under the inconsiderate and unchris-tian treatment of the wealthy in their community. Since James has counseled these poor to be patient and to wait for the deliverance of God, Reicke's insight may very well be accurate.

The word "swear" doesn't refer primarily to the use of profanity (3:9). The point at issue in verse 12 is the taking of an oath, invoking the name of God in order to reinforce the truthfulness of what one has said. Everything we say should be truthful, so something shouldn't be more truth-ful because we attach God's name to it. At times this is like saying "I cross my heart and hope to die" or when you were a kid having your fingers crossed behind your back or saying "I swear on my mother's grave." It seems people have a need to add a few extra words to strengthen what they are say-ing or to invoke some supernatural power to support what they are saying. In a court of law the crime of perjury is still regarded as extremely serious, even in a secular world.

> **Honesty may boost your health, suggests a study that found telling fewer lies benefits people physically.**
>
> Each week for 10 weeks, 1,110 people aged 18 to 71 took a lie detector test and completed health and relationship measures assessing the number of major and minor lies they told that week, says lead author Anita Kelly, a psychology professor at the University of Notre Dame in Indiana. She presented findings at the annual meeting of the American Psychological Association.

> "When they went up in their lies, their health went down," Kelly says. "When their lies went down, their health improved."
>
> —Sharon Jayson, "Avoiding lies can improve health," *USA Today*, August 6, 2012.

Here James is fully in line with the teaching of the Old Testament that false swearing and the giving of oaths is forbidden. Leviticus 19:12, for instance, says, "Do not swear falsely by my name and so profane the name of your God. I am the Lord" (see also Jeremiah 5:2; Hosea 4:2; and Malachi 3:5). We need to say what we mean and mean what we say.

But the issue is not entirely without wrinkles. In Genesis 22:16 God swears by his own name (Hebrews 6:13-18). In the passage from Leviticus just cited, "false swearing" is prohibited, leaving "truthful swearing" an open question. In the Ten Commandments the taking of an oath is not strictly prohibited, but oath-taking is limited to those which one can accomplish (Exodus 20:7). Here too the issue is to avoid invoking the name of God in an oath that is false. God, after all, is the one whose words always accomplish his purpose (Isaiah 55:11). Human beings, on the other hand, utter words that "will not stand up" (Isaiah 8:10), and that "fall to the ground" (1 Samuel 3:19).

To invoke God's name falsely, then, is to involve God in a falsehood. The problem is that sometimes human beings utter falsehoods knowingly, but at other times we are unable to accomplish what we intend. The prohibition recognizes this, and serves to limit and to exclude these unintentional unfortunate remarks. Certainly the Old Testament reveals a developing problem with conscious falsehood (Jeremiah 5:2). But there are still other wrinkles on the matter. In Exodus 22:10-11 an oath "before the Lord" is demanded, the point being that such an oath ensures the truthfulness of testimony.

It seems, in other words, that the point was to avoid

using the name of the Lord in an oath, because human beings are incapable of assuring that what they promise will come true. This makes sense in the context in James, as James has recently argued that such "certainty" is a sign of godless *hybris* (James 4:13-17). But in the case of testimony concerning past events, the name of the Lord serves as a guarantor of truthfulness.

Judaism developed the idea that the best policy was, therefore, to avoid the use of the name of God in any oath (Sirach 23:9, 11). Jesus seemed to agree, adding in a startling conclusion that such forms of oath-taking are of satanic origin (Matthew 5:34-37). He also criticized the Pharisees for what he regarded as semantic indirectness in the taking of oaths (Matthew 23:16-22).

There is, in fact, a close similarity between James and the teaching of Jesus in Matthew 5:34-37. Matthew's text is peppered with more detail, including every element mentioned by James.

Matthew 5:34-37	James 5:12
Do not swear at all either by heaven, for it is God's throne,	Do not swear— not by heaven,
or by the earth, for it is his footstool,	or by earth
or by Jerusalem, for it is the city of the Great King, And do not swear by your head, for you cannot make even one hair white or black.	or by anything else.
Simply let your 'Yes' be 'Yes' and your 'No,' 'No'; anything beyond this comes from the evil one.	Let your "Yes" be yes and your "No," no, or you will be condemned.

Some see this as evidence of the primitive nature of James, as the Matthean saying is more complex and therefore, so the logic goes, must be later. However, it is just as likely that James is drawing upon a saying of Jesus, and has simply shortened it. Furthermore, the idea that "simple" must mean "primitive" or "early," and "complex" must by necessity mean late is a falsehood, in spite of its enduring appeal.

There are a number of parallels to this formula within Judaism. In the Talmud (*Nedarim* 20a) we read, "Never make a practice of vowing, for ultimately you will trespass in the matter of oaths." Josephus writes in reference to the Essenes, "Every statement of theirs is surer than an oath; and with them swearing is avoided, for they think it worse than perjury. For they say that he who is untrustworthy except when he appeals to God, is already under condemnation" (*Antiquities*, 15:10).

> Should we take oaths in court? The oaths forbidden here are those used in casual conversation, not formal oaths taken in a court of law. Legal oaths are intended to bind those who make them. Perjury is a serious offense. Most scholars conclude that James does not require us to refuse to take oaths in court. The swearing that so irritated Jesus and James made a mockery of the truth.
>
> —*Life Application Bible*, 133.

Why does James offer this counsel? 1) To avoid the situation of Jephthah, who swore an oath that bound him to disastrous consequences (Judges 11:30-39); 2) to ensure that Christians are not influenced by pagan oath-swearing formulae; 3) to maintain a high standard of truth in all speech (avoid half-truths, lies, and omissions of the truth); and 4) to avoid involving God in a falsehood if, by chance, what we intend we are unable to accomplish. The consequence for each of these is to fall under the judgment of condemnation, and this James wants us to avoid.

> I see in all this an exhortation to simplicity of speech. Respond to circumstances with a simple "yes" or "no." Answer succinctly and with authenticity. When it comes to the tough circumstances of life, we are wise to avoid long explanations, detailed excuses, and especially pious spiritualizing. This kind of overanalysis leads to stumbling in our words. We will find ourselves bringing God into circumstances to play a role on our terms.
>
> —Swindoll, *New Testament Insights on James, 1 and 2 Peter*, 115.

READ BETWEEN THE LINES

- Is there any significance in James writing "Above all"?
- Why would people swear by heaven or by earth or by anything else when speaking?
- What does James say about swearing?
- Why does James place oath taking here?
- Why would people take an oath instead of simply saying "yes" or "no"?

WELCOME TO MY WORLD

- What kind of message does my swearing (especially using God's name) express to nonbelievers?
- Does this mean we should not take an oath in court today?
- Am I person of my word?
- Would my friends describe me as a truthful person?

The Prayer of Faith

The most obvious feature of this section may seem to be healing, more specifically the prayer over and anointing of the sick (verse 15). But, the heart of this passage, the true theme is prayer (verse 16). The entire section is focused on issues involving prayer, as prayer is mentioned in every verse. James here deals with the prayer of the individual (verse 13), the prayer of the elders (verses 14-15), the prayers of friends and companions for one another (verse 16), and finally the prayer of the righteous prophet Elijah (verses 16-18).

> To someone with no idea of God, of there being a world other than what we can touch and see, prayer looks at best like an odd superstition and at worst like a serious self-deception. Fancy just talking to yourself and thinking it will make a difference to anything! But almost all human traditions, right across history and culture, have been aware of other dimensions which seem mysteriously to intersect with our own...Heaven and earth meet when, in the spirit, someone calls on the name of the Lord... so that the person praying stands with one foot in the place of trouble, sickness and sin and with the other foot in the place of healing, forgiveness and hope. Prayer then brings the latter to bear on the former.
>
> —N. T. Wright, *The Early Christian Letters for Everyone*, 41-42.

James 5:13a

¹³Is anyone among you in trouble? Let them pray.
Is anyone happy? Let them sing songs of praise.

The first issue raised is that of "trouble," suffering in difficult circumstances (verse 13a). This clearly forms a bridge from 5:7-11. We also see here how James is bringing his letter to a close, as this theme formed the first issue raised in the letter (1:2). James is well aware that life, and perhaps especially the Christian life, is one in which we experience trouble—and in such a way that we may feel tempted to call the goodness of God and of our fellow human beings into question. In such times James advocates neither anger, nor stoic resignation, for the former poisons the spirit, and the latter dulls the mind. Instead, he advocates prayer. It's a response that allows us to be active and positive, and keeps us in communication with God.

The Greek word for "trouble" here is *kakopatheo*, which means, "to suffer misfortune," and normally it is not used of illness. Peter Davids offers the opinion that the word indicates not a specific distress or misfortune, but rather the "inner experience of having to endure misfortune."

As in chapter 1, James is not advocating a prayer for the removal of the cause of trouble, so much as for the strength to endure the present troublesome situation. Most people go to God as a last resort or option when everything is spinning out of control. James is telling us that in everything we do we must start with prayer. This does not mean God immediately ends the affliction. But, he does promise to provide patience and perseverance with the grace that is needed. Prayer does not always deliver us from trials but it will see us through trials.

At times our hesitancy to embrace pain and loss is wholly understandable, for it is often difficult to discern God's grace. We inhabit a social and cultural world in which a great premium is placed upon the elimination of discomfort. Our whole culture is dedicated to avoiding suffering, or even the thought of it.

But prayer in adversity also urges us to renounce the materialism and the self-centeredness of the world. This has been a constant theme in James, although our culture seems to ignore it.

Another reason that suffering may be the lot of Christians

is that Christ suffered. Paul reminds us that we are to be fellow sufferers with Christ (Colossians 1:20) by "participation in his sufferings" (Philippians 3:10). Jesus prayed in Gethsemane that the cup might be removed, and it was not, yet the Father gave Jesus the strength he needed to go to the cross to die for our sins (Matthew 26:36-45; Mark 14:32-42; Luke 22:39-46).

There is a kind of suffering that is a difficult concept for us to understand, we who share the culture of recliners and ease. Richard Foster in his book *Prayer: Finding the Heart's True Home* notes that we need to find value in suffering. Jesus was a man of sorrows. Christians who speak of "victory" have perhaps missed what Foster calls the "sacrament of suffering." There is a triumph to suffering, Foster says, but it goes *through* suffering, and not *around* it.

Prayer allows us to understand what God is forming in us through this suffering. Sue Monk Kidd writes of an experience she had once while on a spiritual retreat, an experience which exposes our culturally imposed need for frenetic activity which we so glibly confuse with progress:

> One day after morning prayers, I walked to the edge of the pond and sat on the grass. I listened to the wind sigh over the water and tried to be still, to simply be there and wait in the moment. But almost instantly my inner chaos rose up. The need to keep moving, to act, to solve everything overpowered me. I got to my feet.
>
> As I returned to the guest quarters, I noticed a monk, ski cap pulled over his ears, sitting perfectly still beneath a tree. There was such reverence in his silhouette, such tranquil sturdiness, that I paused to watch. He was the picture of waiting.
>
> Later I sought him out. "I saw you sitting beneath the tree—just sitting there so still. How is it that you can wait so patiently in the moment? I can't seem to get used to the idea of doing nothing."
>
> He broke into a wonderful grin. "Well, there's the problem

> right there, young lady. You've bought into the cultural myth that when you're waiting you're doing nothing."
>
> Then he took his hands and placed them on my shoulders, peered straight into my eyes and said, "I hope you'll hear what I'm about to tell you. I hope you'll hear it all the way down to your toes. When you're waiting, you're *not* doing nothing. You're doing the most important something there is. You're allowing your soul to grow up. If you can't be still and wait, you can't become what God created you to be."
>
> —Sue Monk Kidd, *When the Heart Waits. Spiritual Direction for Life's Sacred Questions*, Harper, San Francisco, 1990, 21-22.

The wisdom of this monk is clear. Prayerful contemplation allows us to slow down, to let our "soul grow up," and catch a glimpse of God's purpose in allowing us to experience affliction. But we are not good at waiting. We are not good at being still before God. When we wait before God, as James says, he allows us to see what he is forming in us. Prayer is the necessary discipline.

Then James discusses the case of those who are happy. The word he uses (*euthymeo*) conveys something far more than the superficial happiness dependent upon circumstance. Rather, it refers to a deeply rooted happiness, a "contentment of the heart," as Douglas Moo puts it. James is referring to the believer who, through prayer, can be in good spirits even when transitory conditions are difficult because of a deep-seated trust in the trustworthiness of God. The word translated "sing songs of praise," (*psallo*) originally meant "to play the harp." It is used frequently in the Psalms, as one would expect (Psalm 33:2; 98:4-5; and 149:3). Our songs of praise are directed to God; singing is actually another form of prayer.

In this verse of "trouble" and being "happy" it's not unlikely that James has in mind the psalms of lament, which feature an honest questioning of God that seems to border on doubt, but which always conclude with a statement of praise and trust. The Psalmist may feel abandoned: "But now you have rejected and humbled us" (Psalm 44:9); but always this "doubt" is in the context of the covenant relationship, "Rise up and help us, rescue us because of your unfailing love" (Psalm 44:26). James likewise wants his readers to remember that God desires and deserves our prayers and praise in both difficult and pleasant times. God wants to talk to us, listen to us, and be with us under all circumstances and at all times.

James 5:14

¹⁴Is anyone among you sick? Let them call the elders of the church to pray over them and anoint them with oil in the name of the Lord.

Having dealt with two occasions for prayer, James now turns to a third, illness. The word for "sick" is *astheneo*, which has a wide range of meanings having to do with weakness of any kind (mental, physical, spiritual, conscience). But as Peter Davids points out, there are reasons for concluding that *astheneo* here is narrower in meaning, specifically that is, physical illness.

The sick person should call the elders of the congregation to come and pray over him and to anoint him with oil. James clearly places the responsibility for initiating the process on the sick person not on the church leadership. There is humility required when someone asks for help. That is part of the attitude God wants us to have when we go into prayer. *Proskaleomai* ("to call") suggests that the situation is dire and requires measures that are somewhat extreme. The word "elders" is used in the Gospels to refer to Jewish leaders in the synagogue, but throughout the remainder of the New Testament it signifies leaders in the Christian church

(Acts 11:30; 1 Timothy 5:17-19, and 1 Peter 5:1). The entire group of these local leaders is to be called.

James knows nothing of a particular person known as a "faith healer," as was recognized by Paul in the Corinthian church (1 Corinthians 12:9, 28, 30). That is, we are not dealing with an example of "faith healing" here. Rather, the act of prayer and anointing for healing is undertaken by the recognized leaders of the church. In 5:13 the person in "trouble" is urged to pray for himself or herself; here the sick person is asked to call others to minister.

The sick person is to be "prayed over." To pray for healing was not unknown within Judaism (Psalm 35:13; 41:4). The main verb is "pray," with "anointing" being a participle and therefore holding a subordinate place to prayer. Regarding the anointing, the grammar is not clear whether the oil is to be applied before or during the prayer, and the timing is probably of little importance. It is also unclear if hands are to be laid upon the sick person. The absence of any clear direction to "lay hands on" the sick person is surprising, given the practice of Jesus (Mark 6:5) and his followers (Acts 9:17). Of course, the "laying on of hands" might be presupposed in the application of oil.

It is obvious that the basis for this action is the firm belief that God is the source of healing, and the anointing is done "in the name of the Lord." There are four possibilities as to the precise implication of this phrase. It could mean 1) calling on the name of the Lord (Luke 10:17), or 2) an appeal to the power associated with the name of the Lord (Acts 3:6), or 3) one who has been commissioned by the Lord (Galatians 1:1, 15), or 4) those consciously assembled as a Christian community (1 Corinthians 5:4). Ultimately, it matters little, for the point is that the Lord is at work in the actions of the elders, who are God's representatives. Any healing is due to the power and action of God, not to any human effort.

As in the previous section, "the Lord" must be Jesus. This tells us that although James is nearly without a discernible Christology, what Christology he does possess is high (see also James 5:7-11).

Anointing the sick with oil is mentioned twice elsewhere in the New Testament. In Luke 10:34 Jesus, in relating the parable of the Good Samaritan, says that the Samaritan bandaged the wounds of the man left for dead by the robbers, "pouring on oil and wine."

The other reference is Mark 6:13, something of a classic standard for modern "faith healers." Mark tells us that the disciples anointed the sick with oil.

Some scholars see the anointing as symbolic of God's unceasing interest in his people that what God deemed best for Israel was not always what Israel deemed best. With this background in view, the anointing mentioned here is not done with a certainty that God will heal, but with the certainty that God cares. To pray with certainty that God will heal seems to disregard one of the prominent themes of James' letter, namely to endure difficulties because God can use them to bring about his purpose in our lives.

Other scholars see this anointing as practical and medicinal. Olive oil was thought to bear medicinal powers of wide application in the ancient world, including to cleanse and soothe wounds (Isaiah 1:6; Luke 10:34). A hot oil bath was tried by Herod to heal a variety of internal and external ailments (Josephus, *Antiquities*, 17:172); and Pliny tells us that oil was used to treat the gums and teeth, to keep the body supple, to neutralize "all poisons," to restore vigor if fatigued, as a laxative, and that when mixed with honey it could improve vision (Pliny, *Natural History*, 23.39-40).

The use of both prayer and anointing oil perhaps indicates the church should seek to come to the aid of both the physical and spiritual needs of a sick person. It would seem James has no conflict between prayer and medicine.

James 5:15

15And the prayer offered in faith will make the sick person well; the Lord will raise them up. If they have sinned, they will be forgiven.

Whatever the precise definition and meaning of the act of anointing, it is the "prayer offered in faith," *not* the anointing, which makes the sick person well (verse 15). This is a point frequently missed in the intricacies of the matter of anointing. The emphasis is placed upon a prayer which expresses trust in God, and that flows from a deep commitment to God (vv. 17-18). The prayer and the faith is, evidently, that of the elders, since only the prayer of the elders is mentioned. It is possible that the sick person's faith is exercised in calling the elders.

This prayer carries with it two results: 1) The sick person is made well (*sozo*); and 2) The Lord will raise him up (*egeiro*). The verb *sozo* is most often used in the New Testament in reference to eschatology and the salvation of believers, and this may be the intent of language here (which implies the resurrection "will raise him up"). Because of this, a number of commentators see this issue as about spiritual death, not physical health. However, the verb "to be healed" (*iaomai*) in 5:16 is normally reserved for physical healing, but can be used for spiritual healing.

The chief issue, then, is whether the future verbs "to make well," "to raise up," and "to be forgiven" refer to eschatological and therefore spiritual healing, or to physical healing. While these verbs can be made to bear eschatological nuance, the weight of the grammatical and lexical evidence is on the side of a physical understanding of the passage. After all, the person about whom this is written is still alive!

While it is possible that James has both in view, it is difficult to escape the conclusion that at the very least he is speaking of physical healing of an illness. To avoid this conclusion on the basis of a predetermined theology does injustice to the text. On the other hand, James has counseled patience in the face of affliction. The key to resolving this apparent dilemma is found in the discerning prayer of the elders.

> There is no authority here for the Romanist "sacrament of extreme unction," which consists in anointing with consecrated oil, one who is about to die. But in these verses the anointing is in view of the sick man's coming back to health, not preparation for death.
>
> —H. A. Ironside, *Expository Notes on the Epistle of James*, 61.

James 5:16a

16aTherefore confess your sins to each other and pray for each other so that you may be healed.

In the first sentence of verse 16, the "therefore" links with the previous verse 15. James implies that sin can cause sickness. This is sound New Testament teaching (John 5:14; Mark 2:5-11), fully in harmony with the remainder of the New Testament. But the New Testament does not teach that all sickness is the result of sin (John 9:1-3), or that all sin causes sickness, or that God always desires to remove sicknesses from troubling us.

In 2 Corinthians 12:7-10 Paul discusses his "thorn in [the] flesh" which he calls a "messenger of Satan." He relates that he prayed to be relieved of this affliction. Paul was a man of unquestioned faith yet Paul says that God had allowed this affliction in order to keep him humble. Paul classified it as a "weakness" which he was glad to bear, for his weakness allowed Christ's power to be evident in him. What was apparently a physical affliction was used by God for a spiritual purpose. What is more, Paul, as a result of prayer, understood it in this fashion. He was able to bear the affliction because God revealed to him its purpose. This is precisely the point that James made in 1:5 (see also Hebrews 11:32-40). Not everyone we pray for will be healed.

> A physician who is also a devout Christian confided that over the years he had grown tired of and even angry about the pastors who enter the rooms of patients with a too smug false surety and confidence. "Often, not always, but often," he said, "they promise a good deal more than gets delivered." His heart is for the patients whose faith may waver as a result. These pastors, he believes, have yet to understand the "sacrament of suffering."
>
> —David

Richard Foster says that there are any number of reasons why healing does not take place. Heading the list is the possibility that we have misinterpreted the focus of our prayer when the Spirit prompts us to pray. Others include a failure to use the available medical resources because we do not wish to see medical science as an avenue God can use for healing. Perhaps we have not prayed specifically enough. In any event, Foster wisely directs us away from laying the blame on the patient and urges us always to act with compassion, being sensitive to the pain and weakened state of the patient.

James clearly teaches that sickness which is caused by sin can be alleviated through public confession and prayer for healing. The fact that elders are not mentioned here does not necessarily indicate that a new case is in view, but rather supports the idea that the prayer of faith pertains to elders and to others as well.

James places great emphasis on confession and community. We are to confess our sins first of all to the Lord (1 John 1:9). James tells us to confess our sins to each other and to pray for one another. Here surfaces his passion for true spiritual community, as seen also in his use of the term "brothers and sisters" throughout the letter. James is instructing us to make amends with those whom we have wronged and forgive those who have wronged us.

James asks us to confess to each other publicly for at least two reasons. 1) It is the practice of vulnerability. The church to which James wrote was rife with arrogance, power politics, and dissension. In order to combat these forces James here urges public vulnerability. The practice of vulnerability and confession will cool tempers and help to heal the divisions within the church. James is advocating the model of Jesus, to become the servant and to become vulnerable before others. As well, 2) confession of wrongs committed against sisters and brothers is a sure path to interpersonal healing.

We are to confess our sins to the Lord (1 John 1:9), but we must also confess them to those who have been affected by them. We must never confess sin beyond the circle of that sin's influence. Private sin requires private confession; public sin requires public confession. As Warren W. Wiersbe has written, it is wrong for Christians to "hang dirty wash in public," for such confessing might do more harm than the original sin.

> Confession helps us to *avoid* sin, Proverbs 28:13 says, "He that covereth his sins shall not prosper: but whoso confesseth and forsaketh them shall have mercy."...It is said confession is good for the soul but bad for the reputation, and a bad reputation makes life more difficult in relation to those close to us, we all know. But closeness and confession force out evildoing.

James 5:16b-18

16bThe prayer of a righteous person is powerful and effective. 17Elijah was a human being, even as we are. He prayed earnestly that it would not rain, and it did not rain on the land for three and a half years. 18Again he prayed, and the heavens gave rain, and the earth produced its crops.

In verse 16b James introduces a new line of thought, the example of the righteous person. The prayer of a righteous person, says James, is both "powerful and effective." The "righteous person" is the one who is committed to doing God's will and to cultivating a relationship with God that knows God's heart. This prayer has a powerful effect. Such a prayer can have noticeable consequences on a person whose sickness is the result of sin, as long as (or especially if) the sin has been confessed. The Greek word for "effective" is *energeo*, from which we get the word "energy."

Howard Hendricks informs us that James was nicknamed by the early church "camel knees" because his knees were so calloused from spending so much time on them in prayer. James was a practitioner not a theorist when it came to prayer. But, who was his role model, his example, his pattern? James has already made reference to three Old Testament examples (Abraham, Rahab, and Job). To this list of Old

Testament examples James now adds a fourth, the prophet Elijah to whom he appeals as an example of a person of prayer. For Elijah prayer was a function of his faith and his trust in God, even in the face of difficult situations.

Perhaps you are thinking, *Why choose Elijah as a pattern for my prayer life? I mean, he was a mighty prophet of God and a worker of miracles; he is certainly in a different league than any of us.* However, James tells us in verse 17 that Elijah was a man "like us" (*homoipathes hemin*), an expression that conveys the sense of having the same limitations. As Swindoll has written, "Elijah was sinful, inconsistent, imperfect, yet forgiven and equipped with gifts from above." Elijah was cut out of the same bolt of human cloth as all of us. Luke uses this same term in Acts 14:15 when Barnabas and Paul attempt to convince the citizens of Lystra that they are not divine beings, but people just like anyone else.

James' point is that such a prayer is possible for the people he is addressing. The phrase "prayed earnestly," is a Semitism, conveying the sense of intense prayer. Elijah passionately poured out his heart to God. Because he was a man of sincere faith, he discerned God's heart and his prayers were honored by God.

James is referring to the account given in 1 Kings 17-18. This Old Testament book does not tell us specifically that Elijah prayed for rain to cease and then for rain to start again, but his praying is implied throughout the story (for example: his prayer for the widow's son in 1 Kings 17:20-24 and for fire to come from heaven in 18:36-37). James may have been familiar with the extra biblical literature such as Ecclesiasticus 48:1-3, so that James, under the influence of the Holy Spirit, authenticated the historical record.

The reference to "three and a half years" is surprising, because 1 Kings 18:1 mentions simply that the drought ended "in the third year." Likely James, similar to Luke (Luke

4:25), is reflecting apocalyptic symbolism in which "three and a half" is a number of sinister omen since it is half of the number seven, the perfect number (Daniel 7:25; Revelation 12:6, 14; 13:5) .

James concludes with the thought that just as the prayer of the righteous Elijah resulted in the refreshing of the earth, so the prayer of the righteous believer can result in the refreshing and healing of a Christian afflicted by sickness caused by sin.

The prayer of the righteous person is powerful because the righteous person has discerned God's leading already. Such wise saints are found in every congregation, and deserve the careful attention of church leadership.

But patient supplication is also beneficial in that God rewards the persistence of the widow who prays day and night (Luke 18:1-8). Elijah is singled out because his heart was sensitive to God. The point here is that sin hinders our ability to pray. God certainly hears the prayers of the sinful, but sin dulls our sensitivity to God, and we become less and less in tune with him. This is what James meant in 4:3 when he scolded his brothers and sisters for asking wrongly.

When I think of prayer I think of Mrs. Elizabeth Dolan. When I knew her she was in her 80s. She was an active member of the church where I served as youth minister for 22 years. She scared me. She was six feet tall and would peer down at me always asking me all kinds of questions. How certain students were doing spiritually or physically or socially. She seemed to be aware of everything going on around her. I would ask her how she came to know all these things and she would peer down on me and say in a commanding voice, "I know everything" and then a "got ya" smile would appear on her face.

She told such wonderful stories. She had a fascinating life. She spent three days with Helen Keller in her home. She tells of going to school in the Northwest in an oxcart. She told of winters when the pond would freeze over and how she would dig into the ice to create a hole in order to baptize people. She was a member of the missions committee at the church and she had a love for kids. But, most important she was a prayer warrior. I can remember my students going to her home just to have her pray with and for them. I have heard dozens of stories of how students' lives were changed simply by praying with her.

—Les

READ BETWEEN THE LINES

- How would a humble and patient person respond to the challenges of life?
- What does "trouble" include?
- How inclusive is the word "sick"?
- Who is to call the elders?
- What does "in the name of the Lord" mean?
- What does "the Lord will raise them up" refer to?
- Why the reference to sins being forgiven in relationship to sickness?
- What is the relationship between confessing sins and prayer that brings healing?
- Is it ever appropriate to confess sins before a group of people?
- What does it mean to be a "righteous" person?
- How is Elijah an example of someone who prayed?

WELCOME TO MY WORLD

- Who taught me to pray? Explain.
- How do I pray when praying for the sick?
- Think of someone I know who has experienced God's healing.

- What makes me happy?
- What is one hymn or song that I like to sing? Explain.
- When has it been hard for me to accept God's answer to one of my prayers?
- What comes to my mind when I think of faith healers and healing?
- How do I feel about sharing my sins with another believer?
- How comfortable am I with hearing another Christian's confession and praying for that person?
- Why do many people go to a bar to confess their sins instead of a church?
- How do I feel about calling the elders of the church to pray for me?
- How does it make me feel to know Elijah was a human being just like me?

The Forgiveness of God

James 5:19-20

[19]My brothers and sisters, if one of you should wander from the truth and someone should bring that person back, [20]remember this: Whoever turns a sinner from the error of their way will save them from death and cover over a multitude of sins.

In this concise conclusion James returns to the themes of sin and forgiveness. In so doing he reveals his pastoral heart. The passage is related to the previous section in that forgiveness follows confession. His opponents in the church have misappropriated to themselves the right to teach, and to teach a doctrine clearly at odds with the Jesus tradition, a tradition James knows.

In its effects this false teaching is savagely corrosive of the true faith. It exalted a brazen anti-law (Torah) spirit pervasive enough to dismiss even the Great Commandment, and claims that "faith" is separate from any particular practical ethic. It also extols the values of Roman provincial society. In so doing it has portrayed the Christian church as one among the many, and therefore an avenue for social climbing and social stratification for the scores who were not (or only marginally) included in the broader political and social life of the civic community. Yet to these purveyors of malicious doctrine, James holds out the hand of forgiveness, and encourages others in the Christian church to win them back to the true faith. Here is a model of the very teaching he has put forward. This is an apt conclusion, for the entire letter is written to turn and prevent people from error.

The passage is short, in fact a single sentence. But it should not be missed that in this one sentence James presents no less than three significant theological ideas.

1) Christians have the opportunity and the responsibility to care for one another through the task of loving doctrinal and moral correction. The theme here is not evangelism, but the care and maintenance of the Christian community. 2) The penalty for sin is death. James will not be evasive on this. 3) In this process the agent of reconciliation "covers" a multitude of sins.

The usual Pauline concluding elements (greetings and personal comments to individuals with whom he is familiar, as well as a benediction) are not in the arsenal of James. Instead, he ends with an exhortation to seek out those who in teaching and practice have wandered from the truth. This implies, of course, an exhortation to avoid disobedience.

As he has frequently done, James employs the phrase "my brothers and sisters" to remind his readers of his relationship to them, a relationship marked by warm interpersonal regard and by a shared status before God. In issuing the call to urge Christians to seek and save those wandering, James aptly sums up the core thrust of the letter. The many particular errors he has catalogued (misuse of the tongue, jealousy, desire for social status at the expense of brothers and sisters in the faith, argumentative, false teaching concerning faith and works) can be summed up as markers of wandering ways. That James is directing this conclusion to the Christian community does not come out strongly enough in the NIV, which renders *tis en humin* with "one of you"; it probably should be translated as "one among you."

The word used for "wander" is *planethe*, which can also mean "lead astray." The implication is that this "wandering" is not wholly innocent. The wanderer may understand that the path chosen is a deviant path, or if the wanderer has pursued the path accidentally or unconsciously, those teaching and practicing this error are certainly conscious of it as different from the truth that they know. The term conjures up a rich array of Old Testament references, most having to do with transgression of the law, and more particularly with idolatry (Proverbs 14:8; Isaiah 9:15-16; Jeremiah 23:17; Ezekiel 33:19). It is possible this deliberate waywardness James sees as somehow influenced by Satan. He has already made reference to this possibility (James 3:15; 4:7), and such teaching is in agreement with the witness of the New Testament generally (Romans 1:27; Ephesians 4:14; 1 Peter 2:25).

The wanderer has wandered from "the truth" (*aletheia*). For James truth is not simply something believed, but also and necessarily something practiced. It is much closer to our English word "conviction." The Bible reflects this in its partiality to speak of truth as a way to go, a path to be followed, the "way of... truth" (Psalm 26:3; Matthew 22:16). And the wanderer is not left to his or her own devices; the burden of reclamation is laid on the community. In this James has much in common with Paul in 2 Corinthians 5:18-21. While Paul seems to be referring to the initial conversion and James to a second turning back to God, both are "conversions." James instructs the church as a whole to seek and save the lost and the wandering.

James concludes his letter in a surprisingly abrupt fashion (5:20). The person who "turns" the errant wanderer saves the wanderer from sins. The Greek word James uses for "turn" is *epistrepho*. The idea here probably owes its origin to two passages in Ezekiel. The first is Ezekiel 33:11, "Say to them, 'As surely as I live, declares the Sovereign LORD, I take no pleasure in the death of the wicked, but rather that they turn from their ways and live. Turn! Turn from your evil ways! Why will you die, people of Israel?'"

The other passage is Ezekiel 34, in which vilification is called down upon the false shepherds of Israel, and God as the true shepherd is extolled. One of the functions God assigns to himself is that of seeking and saving those who wander. Further, God will appoint for Israel a true shepherd, his servant David, who will carry out the same tasks. Thus, those who seek and save the wandering are truly the people of God, for they are like God. "Death" (*thanatou*) here is, of course, spiritual death. Consistent with the teaching of the Bible generally, this death has eternal consequences (Deuteronomy 30:19; Job 8:13).

> To see someone wandering off in a dangerous direction and do nothing about it is a tragic dereliction of duty. It may be hard to turn them back—they may insist they are right and we are wrong!—but the effort must be made, precisely in the humility and patience which James has been urging all through. When that is done, a bit of heaven arrives on earth; a bit of God's future becomes real in the present. New life and forgiveness are there in person.
>
> —**N. T. Wright,** *The Early Christian Letters for Everyone*, **43.**

When we come to the phrase "cover over a multitude of sins" we enter a difficult landscape. Certainly the idea here is to forgive sins. The action of the high priest on the Day of Atonement was to cover (*kaphar* or *kippur*) the sins of the people by sprinkling blood on the atonement cover, the lid of the ark (Leviticus 16:15-16), and James is drawing on that image. What is not so clear is the identity of the one who is saved from death and the one whose sins are covered. The NIV has made an exegetical decision on the first matter, clearly indicating that it is the wanderer who is saved from death. This is a sound decision theologically, as it agrees with the thrust of James and with the theology of Ezekiel. It is also a good decision grammatically, although the grammar would also support the idea that the one saving the wanderer is also saved by that action.

It is likely that James intends the "covering" of the sins of both the wanderer and the one who saves the errant party. We also should not forget that James lays responsibility for the wanderer on the Christian community generally. In fact, this is just one example of the sort of mutual care and responsibility James expects of all within the Christian community.

James ends his letter abruptly by reminding his readers that the wise person walks with God in wisdom, in copying of God and his wisdom. Sin is a problem both corporate and personal. It is subtle and tenacious and dangerous; it should not be underestimated. Christians have a responsibility to their world, and to one another.

James calls us to recognize sin *and* to forgive the sinner with warm welcome. James calls us to moral purity and to maintain a heart of forgiveness. When we do so, we are the true children of God, combining both faith and actions in the fashion James has taught. James invites us to enter into this love relationship with God, and to learn what it means to live in the Spirit.

The teaching of James throughout his letter is often harsh and even rigid. But then, so was the mandate given by Jesus. But here at the end of his letter James allows the note of grace, a soft note that has sounded through most of the letter, to ring out loud and true. Forgiveness must be offered, but it is balanced with faith which is active, which has captured mind and heart and body.

READ BETWEEN THE LINES

- Do Christians have a duty to bring back those who have wandered away from the faith?
- How are we responsible for one another?
- How can we help people without being busybodies?

WELCOME TO MY WORLD

- Have I wandered from the faith? Explain.
- Who or what brought me back?
- How have I reached out to those who have wandered?

BIBLIOGRAPHY

Adamson, James B. *The Epistle of James*. NICNT. Grand Rapids: Eerdmans, 1976.

Barrett, Ethel. *Will the Real Phony Please Stand Up?* Glendale, CA: G/L Publications, 1969.

Barton, Bruce B. et al. *Life Application Bible Commentary: James*. Wheaton, IL: Tyndale House Publishers, 1992.

Bickel, Bruce and Stan Jantz. *James: Working Out Your Faith*. Eugene, OR: Harvest House Publishers, 2008.

Blomberg, Craig L., and Mariam J. Kamell. *Exegetical Commentary on the New Testament*. Ed. Clinton E. Arnold. Grand Rapids, MI: Zondervan, 2008.

Courson, Jon. *Jon Courson's Application Commentary: New Testament*. Nashville, TN: Thomas Nelson, Inc. 2003.

Davids, Peter H. *The Epistle of James: A Commentary on the Greek Text*. NICGT. Grand Rapids: Eerdmans, 1982.

Davids, Peter H. *James: Good News Commentary*. San Francisco: Harper and Row, 1983.

Guthrie, George H. and Douglas J. Moo. *Zondervan Illustrated Bible Backgrounds Commentary: Hebrews, James*. Grand Rapids, MI: Zondervan, 2002.

Harrison, Paul V., and Robert E. Picirilli. *The Randall House Bible Commentary: James, 1, 2 Peter and Jude*. Ed. Robert E. Picirilli. Nashville TN: Randall House Publications, 1992.

Hendricks, Howard G. *The Battle of the Gods*. Chicago: Moody Press, 1972.

Hiebert, D.E. *The Epistle of James: Tests of a Living Faith*. Chicago: Moody Press, 1979.

Hughes, Kent R. *James: Faith That Works*. Wheaton, IL: Crossway Books, 1991.

Ironside, H. A. *Expository Notes on the Epistle of James and Peter*. Loizeaux Brothers, 1947.

Laws, Sophie. *The Epistle of James*. Black's New Testament Commentaries. Peabody, Mass: Hendrickson, 1980.

Lenski, R.C.H. *The Epistle to the Hebrews and the Epistle of James*. Minneapolis, MN: Augsburg Publishing House, 1963.

MacArthur, John. *The MacArthur New Testament Commentary: James*. Chicago, IL: Mood Publishers, 1998.

Martin, Ralph P. *Word Biblical Commentary: James*. Ed. David A. Hubbard, Glen W. Barker. Nashville, TN: Word, Incorporated, 1988.

Martin, Ralph P. *James*. WBC. Waco, Texas: Word, 1988.

McCartney, Dan G. *Baker Exegetical Commentary on the New Testament: James*. Grand Rapids, MI: Baker Academic, 2009.

McKnight, Scot. *The New International Commentary on the New Testament: The Letter of James*. Grand Rapids, MI: Wm. B. Eerdmans Publishing Co, 2011.

Mitton, C.L. *The Epistle of James*. Grand Rapids: Eerdmans, 1966.

Moo, Douglas J. *The Letter of James: The Pillar New Testament Commentary*. Grand Rapids, MI: B. Eerdmans Publishing Co., 2000.

Motyer, J.A. *The Message of James: The Test of Faith*. The Bible Speaks Today. Downers Grove, Illinois: InterVarsity, 1985.

Nystrom, David P. *The NIV Application Commentary: James.* Grand Rapids, MI: Zondervan, 1997.

Robertson, A.T. *Studies in the Epistle of James.* Nashville, TN: Broadman Press.

Ropes, J.H., *A Critical and Exegetical Commentary on the Epistle of St. James.* ICC. Edinburgh: T. & T. Clark, 1916.

Serrão, C. Jeanne Orjala. *James: A Commentary in a Wesleyan Tradition.* Kansas City, MO: Beacon Hill Press, 2010.

Sidebottom, E.M. *James, Jude, 2 Peter.* NCBC. Grand Rapids: Eerdmans, 1982.

Stulac, George M. *James.* The IVP New Testament Commentary Series. Downers Grove, Illinois: InterVarsity, 1993.

Swindoll, Charles R. *Swindoll's New Testament Insights: Insights on James, 1 & 2 Peter.* Grand Rapids, MI: Zondervan, 2010.

Vlachos, Chris A. *James Exegetical Guide to the Greek New Testament.* Nashville, Tennessee: Broadman and Holman Publishing Company, 2013.

Wiersbe, Warren W. *Be Mature, Growing Up in Christ, NT Commentary James.* Colorado Springs, CO: David C. Cook, 1978.

Wilson, Marvin R. *Our Father Abraham: Jewish Roots of the Christian Faith.* Grand Rapids, MI: Wm. B. Eerdmans Publishing Company, 1989.

Wright, N. T. *The Christian Letters for Everyone.* Westminster John Knox Press, Louisville, Kentucky, 2011.

Share Your Thoughts

With the Author: Your comments will be forwarded to the author when you send them to *zauthor@zondervan.com*.

With Zondervan: Submit your review of this book by writing to *zreview@zondervan.com*.

Free Online Resources at
www.zondervan.com

Daily Bible Verses and Devotions: Enrich your life with daily Bible verses or devotions that help you start every morning focused on God. Visit www.zondervan.com/newsletters.

Free Email Publications: Sign up for newsletters on Christian living, academic resources, church ministry, fiction, children's resources, and more. Visit www.zondervan.com/newsletters.

Zondervan Bible Search: Find and compare Bible passages in a variety of translations at www.zondervanbiblesearch.com.

Other Benefits: Register to receive online benefits like coupons and special offers, or to participate in research.